3 EDITION

MANAGING A
DIVERSE WORKFORCE

To the memory of my mother
Zina Powell
a wonderful parent and friend

MANAGING A DIVERSE WORKFORCE

3^{EDITION}

LEARNING ACTIVITIES

Gary N. Powell

University of Connecticut

$SAGE

Los Angeles | London | New Delhi
Singapore | Washington DC

For information:

SAGE Publications, Inc.
2455 Teller Road
Thousand Oaks, California 91320
E-mail: order@sagepub.com

SAGE Publications Ltd.
1 Oliver's Yard
55 City Road
London EC1Y 1SP
United Kingdom

SAGE Publications India Pvt. Ltd.
B 1/I 1 Mohan Cooperative Industrial Area
Mathura Road, New Delhi 110 044
India

SAGE Publications Asia-Pacific Pte. Ltd.
33 Pekin Street #02-01
Far East Square
Singapore 048763

Printed in the United States of America

Library of Congress Cataloging-in-Publication Data

Managing a diverse workforce : learning activities / Gary N. Powell. —3rd ed.
    p. cm.
Includes bibliographical references and index.
ISBN 978-1-4129-9092-9 (pbk.)
    1. Diversity in the workplace. 2. Discrimination in employment. 3. Multiculturalism. 4. Minorities—Employment.
I. Powell, Gary N.

HF5549.5.M5P69 2011
658.3008—dc22

2010035400

This book is printed on acid-free paper.

10 11 12 13 14 10 9 8 7 6 5 4 3 2 1

Acquisitions Editor:	Lisa Cuevas Shaw
Editorial Assistant:	MaryAnn Vail
Production Editor:	Libby Larson
Typesetter:	C&M Digitals (P) Ltd.
Proofreader:	Theresa Kay
Cover Designer:	Candice Harman
Marketing Manager:	Helen Salmon
Permissions Editor:	Karen Ehrmann

Contents

Preface

The purpose of this book is the same as the purpose of the graduate and undergraduate courses I teach on managing a diverse workforce. The goal is for you to be able to answer the following question as many times as possible:

What can I do—in the workplace and in society—to promote the creation of inclusive work environments in which full advantage is taken of the potential contributions of all members, regardless of their job irrelevant personal characteristics and group memberships?

To achieve this goal, the book provides a comprehensive set of learning activities that address issues related to workplace diversity. Participation in these activities will lead to a greater appreciation of the wide range of issues that arise when people classify themselves or are classified by others as members of different groups on whatever basis. Learning how to deal with these issues in a manner that preserves the integrity of all members of the workforce is fostered.

The *third edition* of the book contains the most popular and frequently used activities from the second edition; these activities have been updated to incorporate my classroom experiences with them and those of other instructors. In addition, the book offers several activities that appear for the first time in this edition. Each of these new activities has been pilot-tested in my courses on managing a diverse workforce. I will be interested to hear about *your* experiences with these exercises and any revisions you would like to recommend for future editions.

Here is a run-down of what the learning activities have to offer:

1. They explore the impact of diversity on the basis of numerous personal characteristics, including sex, race, ethnicity, age, physical and mental abilities, national culture, religion, socioeconomic

status, education, sexual orientation, marital status, parental status, family background, and appearance.

2. They cover a wide range of diversity topics. Table 1 provides a list of the general topic(s) addressed by each activity. In addition, many of the activities may be adapted by the instructor to address particular topics not included in this list.

3. They are set in many different types of work settings, including both business and not-for-profit organizations.

This book provides background information, procedure, and discussion questions for each learning activity. A separate instructor's manual provides guidance for instructors on how to conduct the various activities, including masters for handouts.

For their contributions to the preparation of this book, I express my deep gratitude to Tiger the Cat for her loving, affectionate, playful, and distracting presence in my life; and Laura Graves, my wife and favorite colleague, for standing by me and encouraging me all the way.

Table 1   Topics Addressed by Learning Activities

A.	Introduction/Dimensions of Diversity
	    1. Your Pie Chart
	    2. People Like Us

B.	Working With People in the Majority Group 3. Becoming a Minority
C.	Working With People From a Different National Culture 4. Would You Repeat That?

D.	Being Socialized
	    5. Gender-Based Perceptions
	    6. Once Upon a Time

E.	Making Employment Decisions
	    7. Consulting Analyst Wanted
	    8. Who Gets Hired?
	    9. The Prison "Break"

F.	Working in Diverse Teams 9. The Prison "Break"

G.	Promoting Positive Race Relations 10. Beyond O. J.
H.	Leading People 11. Designer Decorations

I.	Dealing With Sexuality in the Workplace
	    12. Dealing With Sexually Oriented Behavior
	    13. Mixing Sex and Work

J.	Managing the Work-Family Interface
	    14. Have I Got Good News for Us!
	    15. Managing From a Distance

K.	Pursuing a Career
	    15. Managing From a Distance
	    16. Networking Role Play

L.	Working as a Non-Family Member in a Family Firm 17. We Are Family

M.	Working With People With Disabilities
	    18. Puzzled Perceptions
	    19. Sara's Acting Strange Lately

N.	Working With People of a Different Age
	    20. The Older Employee
	    21. The College Graduate

O.	Promoting Nondiscrimination 22. Diversity Incidents
P.	Promoting Diversity 23. Affirmative Action at Ole State
Q.	Promoting Inclusion 24. The Inclusive Workplace

1

Your Pie Chart

Purpose:	1. To increase awareness of your own cultural background and how it compares to that of others.
	2. To raise awareness of the importance of self-identity based on affiliations with groups.
	3. To consider the influence of self-identity on individuals' experiences in organizational settings.
Preparation:	None
Time:	30 to 45 minutes

BACKGROUND

Personal characteristics (some changeable, others not), which may influence individuals' basic self-image and sense of identity, may also influence experiences in the workplace. **Primary dimensions of diversity** are essentially unchangeable personal characteristics (e.g., sex, race, ethnicity, age, sexual orientation, physical and mental abilities). **Secondary dimensions of diversity**, on the other hand, are changeable personal characteristics that are acquired and may be modified or abandoned throughout life (e.g., education, income, marital and parental status, religion, political affiliation, work experience). People also distinguish themselves in many other ways, such as in their choices of collegiate fraternities or sororities, hobbies, activities, clothing and grooming style,

AUTHOR'S NOTE: This exercise is reprinted with permission of the publisher. From *Developing competency to manage diversity: Readings, cases and activities,* © 1997 by Taylor Cox, Jr. & Ruby L. Beale, Berrett-Koehler Publishers, Inc., San Francisco, CA. All rights reserved. www.bkconnection.com.

and music. Of course, secondary characteristics are not completely self-determined; educational background, work experience, income, and marital status are affected by others' decisions. However, people generally have more control over secondary dimensions of diversity than over primary dimensions.

Because individuals' sense of identity is influenced by self-selected groups, this exercise examines how people categorize themselves in their group affiliations along the many different dimensions of both types of diversity.

PROCEDURE

1. Working individually, create a pie chart identifying group affiliations that have some importance in your self-concept. These affiliations may be based on any of the primary or secondary dimensions of diversity mentioned above or on some other personal characteristic that is particularly important to you (e.g., cat or dog lover, fan of favorite sports team or musician). Indicate the approximate importance of each group affiliation by the size of the slice of pie that you assign to it. (10 minutes)

2. Participate in a discussion based on the following questions: (remaining time)

   a. What did you learn about yourself?

   b. What surprised you the most?

   c. What group affiliations were mentioned the most?

d. What did you learn about others that surprised you?

e. How does your self-identity influence your experiences in organizational settings?

REFERENCE   Loden, M., & Rosener, J. B. (1991). Chapter 2, Dimensions of diversity. In *Workforce America: Managing employee diversity as a vital resource* (pp. 17–35). Homewood, IL: Business One Irwin.

2

People Like Us

Purpose:

1. To apply concepts of intergroup dynamics to everyday problems that people face.
2. To raise awareness of the underlying group dynamics in organizational settings.
3. To consider the influence of how others categorize them on individuals' experiences in the workplace.

Preparation: None

Time: 60 to 75 minutes

BACKGROUND

Categorizations of others are made along the many different dimensions of diversity, both primary and secondary. When people have little or no experience in working together, initial categorizations, which are likely to be along the highly visible and primary dimensions of diversity such as sex, race, and age, may result in stereotyping, prejudice, and discrimination. A **stereotype** is a set of beliefs about the personal attributes of a group of people. Stereotyping is a cognitive activity, related to thinking, learning, and remembering distinctions between various groups of people. People who display **prejudice**, or a negative attitude toward members of other groups, are engaging in an emotional activity. Finally, **discrimination**, a behavioral activity, is

AUTHOR'S NOTE: This exercise was prepared by Judith A. Neal. © Judith A. Neal. Used with permission.

exhibited in how people treat members of other groups and in what they decide about others.

We have reason to be concerned about all three of these phenomena. All of us may be targets of or engage in stereotyping, prejudice, and discrimination. This exercise examines the effects of how members of different groups are categorized by others on their experiences in the workplace.

PROCEDURE

1. The instructor will guide participants in the formation of discussion groups based on primary dimensions of diversity.

2. As a group, answer the following question: "What are the primary problems that people like us experience in this organizational setting?" Select the three problems that bother you the most. (20 minutes)

3. The instructor will provide instructions for the remainder of the exercise.

REFERENCES

Fiske, S. T. (1998). Stereotyping, prejudice, and discrimination. In D. T. Gilbert, S. T. Fiske, & G. Lindzey (Eds.), *The handbook of social psychology*, vol. 2 (4th ed., pp. 357–411). Boston: McGraw-Hill.

Hunter, T. D. (Ed.) (2009). *Handbook of prejudice, stereotyping, and discrimination*. New York: Psychology Press.

3

Becoming a Minority

Purpose:	1. To expose you to cultural differences between yourself and others in a self-chosen environment that is unfamiliar to you.
	2. To increase understanding of how cultural differences influence feelings of comfort and relationships between people in social settings.

Preparation:	Complete assignment

Time:	30 to 45 minutes

BACKGROUND

If they have a choice, people generally choose to associate with others whom they see as similar to themselves in familiar settings. It can be difficult for students who have grown up in a homogeneous environment to understand and appreciate individuals from backgrounds that are different from their own. However, the demographic composition of the labor force around the world has become more diverse in recent years on the basis of sex, race, ethnicity, and many other primary and secondary dimensions of diversity. As a result, employers whose management practices were once appropriate for a homogeneous group of employees have had to make adjustments to attract and retain talented individuals from diverse groups. Given these changes, most workers will not be effective at their jobs unless they acquire skills in dealing with culturally different coworkers

AUTHOR'S NOTE: This exercise was prepared by Renate R. Mai-Dalton. It is reprinted from Renate R. Mai-Dalton, Exposing business school students to cultural diversity: Becoming a minority, *Organizational Behavior Teaching Review*, Volume 9, Number 3, 1984-5. Used with permission.

as superiors, subordinates, and peers. This exercise gives you the opportunity to personally experience cultural differences in an unfamiliar setting.

PROCEDURE

1. The following assignment will expose you to a new situation, require you to observe your surroundings carefully, and ask you to describe both what you felt and what you think others might have felt to have you among them. Your task is to go to an unfamiliar place and observe what you see. You may go with someone you know, but your focus should be on your own experience and what you make of it. To give you some ideas about possible places to visit, here are examples of previous choices:

    a. A member of a particular religious congregation attended services at a different religious congregation or one that was primarily composed of members of a different race.

    b. A participant with sight visited a school for the blind; one with hearing visited a school for the deaf.

    c. A participant with a particular sexual orientation went to a party primarily attended by people with different sexual preferences.

    d. A participant who was able to walk spent an afternoon at the local mall in a wheelchair.

    e. A participant who did not ordinarily engage in physical exercise spent time in the weight-lifting room at a fitness center.

    f. A younger participant visited a nursing home.

    g. An adult participant played laser tag in an entertainment arena with a group of children.

    h. A woman went to a car auction.

    i. A man went to a party held to sell cookware products.

    j. A woman attended a basketball game between her alma mater and its archrival at the archrival's home arena wearing her school colors.

    There are, of course, many other possibilities. Choose a setting that you sincerely want to learn about; this will allow you to maintain your integrity and justify your visit. Do not choose a setting where you would feel like an intruder into someone's privacy, however, and do not place yourself in a situation that is physically dangerous. If in doubt, check in advance as to whether your presence is acceptable to the group.

2. Briefly describe your experience below:

   a. Date and address where the experience took place:

   b. Length of time spent there:

   c. Brief description of the setting:

   d. Your reaction to the situation in terms of your behavior and feelings:

   e. The reactions of others toward you:

   f. What did this experience teach you about being different from others in your environment?

   g. How might permanently living or working in such a setting influence your development?

3. The instructor will place you in a discussion group of people who have visited similar settings. As a group, discuss what each of you experienced and learned from your experience. (30 minutes)

4. Participate in a general discussion based on the following questions: (remaining time)

   a. What similarities and differences were there between the different settings visited?

   b. What did it feel like to be in the minority?

   c. Did you behave differently from how you normally behave? In what ways?

   d. What are the advantages and disadvantages of putting yourself in a situation where you are in the minority?

   e. How might you behave if you were permanently in a minority position, either where you live or work? How might your motivation to work, study, or otherwise achieve be affected?

4 Would You Repeat That?

Purpose:	1. To demonstrate how cultural differences affect learning in the university classroom.
	2. To examine the impact of accents on teacher-student interactions.
Preparation:	None
Time:	60 to 75 minutes

BACKGROUND

Diversity in the university classroom on the basis of teachers' and students' **national culture** may have an enormous effect on what students learn and how teachers and students interact, both positive and negative. The teacher and students may learn more about each other's national culture, which makes everyone more knowledgeable and well-rounded on cultural differences. In addition, these kinds of interactions prepare students for the increasingly diverse global economy. However, differences in national culture between the teacher and students can have a negative impact in the classroom when handled improperly. For example, a foreign teaching assistant may have an accent that students have trouble understanding, which impedes their learning and leaves them frustrated. The purpose of this exercise is to examine how a teacher's accent affects classroom interactions in colleges and universities.

AUTHOR'S NOTE: This exercise was prepared by Jennifer M. Byrnes, Brad C. Heering, Rebecca L. Patten, and Gary N. Powell.

PROCEDURE

1. In a prior class, the instructor will select a volunteer to play the role of a teaching assistant in a role play of a college class.

2. Review the role description provided by the instructor and prepare to play your role. (10 minutes)

3. The teaching assistant teaches the lesson of the day as students play their own roles. (15 minutes)

4. Participate in a discussion based on the following questions: (remaining time)

   a. Questions for the teaching assistant:

      (1) What were thinking as you saw how the lesson was going?

      (2) How did it make you feel to be unable to communicate something you know so well?

   b. Questions for the students:

      (1) How did it make you feel to make the teaching assistant repeat himself or herself?

      (2) Have you had a college course in which this was an issue? How did you and other students deal with it?

(3) Do you see this as a common classroom issue?

c. General questions:

    (1) Whose responsibility is it to make sure that your learning is not affected by the teacher's accent?

    (2) What are possible solutions to the issues depicted in this role play?

5

Gender-Based Perceptions

Purpose: 1. To increase awareness of gender stereotypes.
2. To increase awareness of your own tendency to stereotype others.
3. To examine the influence of stereotypes on individuals' interactions with others in daily life and work settings.

Preparation: None

Time: 60 to 75 minutes

BACKGROUND

Stereotyping, or mentally grouping people based on personal characteristics and then assigning traits to members of each group, is a pervasive human phenomenon. Although seemingly harmless at first glance, excessive reliance on stereotypes can cause problems:

1. Stereotyping may lead to prejudice and discrimination. If people did not engage in stereotyping, perhaps they would exhibit more tolerance and understanding toward each other.

AUTHOR'S NOTE: This exercise was prepared by Michael London and Joy A. Schneer. © Michael London and Joy A. Schneer. Used with permission.

2. Although a given stereotype may accurately describe the average member of a group, it rarely applies to all group members. When we stereotype people on the basis of any dimension of diversity (e.g., sex, race, age, education, income), we may overlook them as individuals.

The purpose of this exercise is to examine the influence of gender stereotypes on your perceptions of others. **Gender stereotypes** represent beliefs about the psychological traits that males and females possess. According to gender stereotypes, females are high in **feminine** traits such as compassion, gentleness, and sensitivity to the needs of others, whereas males are high in **masculine** traits such as dominance, independence, and aggressiveness. Gender stereotypes have remained essentially stable over the years despite considerable changes in the social roles of adult men and women. However, as you may discover in this exercise, the fact that people may agree does not mean that stereotypes apply to everyone.

PROCEDURE

1. Find a partner with whom you have had very little contact, preferably a member of the opposite sex. (5 minutes)

2. Complete the Gender-Based Perceptions Worksheet. (20 minutes)

3. Participate in a discussion based on the following questions: (remaining time)

    a. In what ways did you and your partner stereotype each other?

    b. Which of your own stereotypes were challenged?

c. What dimensions of diversity may have influenced your predictions?

d. What stereotypes about members of your own sex affect your interactions with others in daily life and work settings? How do these stereotypes affect you?

e. How do the stereotypes that you hold affect your interactions with others?

REFERENCE   Powell, G. N. (2011). Chapter 3, Becoming women and men. *Women and men in management*, 4th ed. (pp. 38–73). Thousand Oaks, CA: Sage.

GENDER-BASED PERCEPTIONS

WORKSHEET

Instructions:

1. Find a partner with whom you have had very little contact.

2. Record your agreement with each statement on this worksheet according to the following scale (Column 1):

Total	1	2	3	4	5	6	7	8	9	10	Total
Disagreement											Agreement

3. Predict the rating that your partner gave to each statement (Column 3).

4. Share and record your ratings and predictions (Columns 2 & 4).

5. Compute and total the absolute differences between the two sets of ratings and predictions to determine prediction accuracy (Columns 5 & 6).

Column No.	1	2	3	4	5	6
Statement	*Your Own Rating*	*Your Partner's Prediction of Your Rating*	*Your Prediction of Your Partner's Rating*	*Your Partner's Rating*	*Absolute Difference Between 1 & 2: Accuracy of Your Partner's Predictions*	*Absolute Difference Between 3 & 4: Accuracy of Your Predictions*
1. I ask for directions when I am lost.						
2. I find it easy to talk about my feelings.						
3. I make time every day for leisure activities.						
4. I believe that a mother should take a career break to be at home with her young children.						
5. I regularly spend time to get my hair just right.						
6. I avoid movies that have violence in them.						

Column No.	1	2	3	4	5	6
Statement	Your Own Rating	Your Partner's Prediction of Your Rating	Your Prediction of Your Partner's Rating	Your Partner's Rating	Absolute Difference Between 1 & 2: Accuracy of Your Partner's Predictions	Absolute Difference Between 3 & 4: Accuracy of Your Predictions
7. A husband should earn more than his wife.						
8. I don't let people interrupt me when I am talking.						
9. I feel more comfortable talking to men than to women.						
10. Talking on my cell phone is one of my favorite things to do.						
11. My career is the most important thing in my life.						
12. I like to shop at the mall.						
13. I offer advice when someone tells me about a problem.						
14. People should always be nice.						
15. I would not want to have a woman for a boss.						
16. I like to watch sports events.						
17. I like to cook for my friends and family.						
18. I like to wash my car.						
19. I am a good driver.						
20. I am skilled at household repairs.						
21. I go to the doctor when I am ill or in pain.						
22. I like to have a wide selection of shoes.						
23. I hate killing spiders or bugs.						
24. I am good at math.						
					Total =	Total =

6

Once Upon a Time

Purpose: 1. To analyze the prevalence of gender stereotypes in children's fairy tales.
2. To understand how these stereotypes may affect the development of a child's self-identity.
3. To increase awareness of the need for stereotype-free fairy tales that will encourage children to develop less restricted self-identities.

Preparation: None

Time: 60 to 75 minutes

BACKGROUND

Fairy tales influence children's development by providing a richly detailed view, whether realistic or distorted, of human (and animal) experiences and what lessons may be drawn from these experiences. Children are exposed to fairy tales, which often convey stereotypical roles, at a very early age through stories, movies, and television cartoons. For example, Walt Disney's classic 1937 animated film of *Snow White and the Seven Dwarfs*, based on a Brothers Grimm fairy tale, has been re-released several times and is still popular to this day. It depicts Snow White as cheerfully doing

AUTHOR'S NOTE: This exercise was prepared by Amy E. Duncan, Heather L. Stuart, Brian S. Tomko, and Gary N. Powell.

housework, first for the wicked Queen and then for the dwarfs, while singing blissfully about the handsome prince she hopes to marry (and keep house for). The dwarfs are depicted as both personal slobs and as a cohesive group epitomizing teamwork, good humor, and masculine protectiveness; they protect Snow White and, more important, she picks up after them.

The purpose of this exercise is to consider ways to counteract the influence of fairy tale stereotypes on children's development. It will challenge you to create your own modern fairy tale that is stereotype-free.

PROCEDURE

1. Form groups of five to seven members. (5 minutes)

2. As a group, create a fairy tale that is completely free of all stereotypes. Start with the phrase, "Once upon a time . . . " and proceed to write your story, including a moral at the end. (30 minutes)

3. Each group will read its fairy tale, including the moral, to the rest of the class and comment on any obstacles encountered during the task. (5 minutes per group)

4. Participate in a discussion based on the following questions: (remaining time)

   a. What stereotypes were the most difficult to avoid?

   b. Do children need to learn about stereotypes at an early age to prepare them for society? If so, how should this learning be stimulated?

c. How would exposure to nontraditional roles in fairy tales influence the development of children's self-identities?

d. What can teachers and parents do to decrease children's reliance on stereotypes in making sense of their world?

REFERENCES   Disney, R. H. (2003). *Snow White and the seven dwarfs.* Burbank, CA: Golden/Disney.

Snow White and the seven dwarfs (1937). (2009). DVD version. Burbank, CA: Walt Disney Studios Home Entertainment.

7

Consulting Analyst Wanted

Purpose:
1. To gain experience in interviewing and being interviewed.
2. To explore the dynamics of the recruiter-applicant relationship.
3. To examine how treatment and outcome discrimination may be manifested in employment interviews.

Preparation: Read background sheet

Time: 60 to 75 minutes

BACKGROUND

Recruiters, personnel officers, and managers typically have little information on which to base their decisions to hire a particular job applicant. Resumes present some information about backgrounds and experiences but little about personal qualities. Even personal referrals may be misleading because the individuals who refer applicants invariably provide glowing testimonials. Recruiting conducted on college campuses typically consists of interviews that may last no more than 20 to 30 minutes. As screening devices, campus interviews allow organizations to reduce a large number of applicants to a select few who receive closer scrutiny. However, they lead to quickly formed impressions that present only blurred pictures of applicants.

AUTHOR'S NOTE: This exercise was prepared by Gary N. Powell. It was inspired by an exercise prepared by Laura M. Graves and Charles A. Lowe.

Judgments about individuals based on very little data, as when organizations use interviews to make initial screening decisions, may be influenced by stereotypes and result in discrimination. Two kinds of discrimination may occur, **treatment discrimination** in how the interview is conducted and **outcome discrimination** in who get hired and at what salary. The purpose of this exercise is to examine the interview process, paying close attention to how both types of discrimination may be manifested and how to guard against them.

PROCEDURE

1. Prior to class, read the Consulting Analyst Wanted Background Sheet.

2. Half of the participants will play the role of recruiter and half the role of applicant. Two rounds of 15-minute interviews will be held; depending on your role, you will either conduct two interviews or be interviewed twice. After each round of interviews, both recruiters and applicants will complete an interview assessment sheet. After the second round, each recruiter will decide which of the two candidates to hire and will personally deliver a job offer letter to the chosen applicant and a rejection letter to the other applicant. Thus, if you are an applicant, you will receive two, one, or no job offers. The instructor will divide the participants into recruiters and applicants, assign an applicant to each recruiter, and give each recruiter a job offer letter and a rejection letter. (10 minutes)

3. Review the Background Sheet and prepare for your upcoming interviews as recruiter or applicant. (5 minutes)

4. Conduct the first interview. (15 minutes)

5. Complete the Recruiter or Applicant Assessment Sheet for the first interview. (5 minutes)

6. After the instructor assigns a different applicant to each recruiter, conduct the second interview. (15 minutes)

7. Complete the Recruiter or Applicant Assessment Sheet for the second interview. At this time, each recruiter decides which applicant to hire and personally delivers job offer and rejection letters. (5 minutes)

8. After the instructor has collected information from the class about the results of interviews, participate in a discussion based on the following questions. (remaining time)

    a. Questions for recruiters:

        (1) What were good responses to questions you asked? Poor responses?

        (2) What did applicants do to make a good or poor impression?

        (3) What factors did you take into account in making this decision?

    b. Questions for applicants:

        (1) What were good questions asked by recruiters? Poor questions?

        (2) What did recruiters do to make a good or poor impression?

        (3) What do you think was the basis for recruiters' decisions about you? Why do you think you received the number of job offers you did?

   c. General questions:

     (1) Were stereotypes or personal biases displayed in interviews?

     (2) Was there any evidence of treatment discrimination?

     (3) Was there any evidence of outcome discrimination?

     (4) What can organizations do to guard against treatment and outcome discrimination in employment interviews?

     (5) What are the implications of this exercise for an applicant in an interview situation?

CONSULTING ANALYST WANTED

BACKGROUND SHEET

Background: Patterson Consulting, a global management consulting firm, employs over 75,000 professionals in 120 countries. Over the past four years, it has increased revenue an average of 25% a year in the United States alone. Its vision statement declares,

> "Patterson Consulting is committed to quality by having the best people with knowledge capital partner with the best clients to deliver value. Our greatest resources are our people. We offer world-class training, well-planned career paths with advancements based on performance and business needs, above-average compensation and benefits, challenging and exciting work, and plenty of opportunities to succeed."

Looking down from the top of the corporate hierarchy, professionals in Patterson Consulting work as partners, associate partners, managers, consultants, or analysts. Patterson is looking to hire the best undergraduates and MBAs for its entry-level analyst positions, where every new professional employee without significant work experience starts. Analysts develop business skills and knowledge while making significant contributions on consulting projects under the direction of consultants; eventually, high-performing analysts who have acquired the necessary experience supervise and train others. In hiring analysts, Patterson Consulting looks for people who possess a unique combination of problem-solving skills, determination, well-rounded interests, strong communication skills, an ability to excel in a team environment, a dedication to exceeding the client's expectations, and a willingness to travel.

Recruiter's Role: You are a college recruiter for Patterson Consulting. You have been asked to interview two promising applicants at the state university who have been identified through review of resumes and determine which of the two is most suited for an analyst position in the Hartford, Connecticut, office. Both applicants will graduate shortly and have similar internship experience and work experience (mostly part-time). Before the interview, consider what job-relevant skills you are looking for, including whether the applicant's personality seems right for the job.

Applicant's Role: You will be graduating shortly from the state university and are being considered for a position as an analyst by Patterson Consulting. Your outstanding resume has landed you an interview. Now you just need to do well in this interview to get the job, which you really want. Before the interview, consider what skills you have that are relevant to this job and be prepared to make the interviewer aware that you have these skills.

CONSULTING ANALYST WANTED

RECRUITER ASSESSMENT SHEET

How would you describe Applicant #1?	*weak*						*strong*
Communications ability	1	2	3	4	5	6	7
Future potential	1	2	3	4	5	6	7
Personal appearance	1	2	3	4	5	6	7
Personality	1	2	3	4	5	6	7
Future ambitions	1	2	3	4	5	6	7
Maturity	1	2	3	4	5	6	7
Relevant work experience	1	2	3	4	5	6	7
Knowledge about company	1	2	3	4	5	6	7

How did the interview with Applicant #1 go?	*disagree*						*agree*
Applicant was able and willing to answer any questions.	1	2	3	4	5	6	7
Applicant tried hard to show interest in the job.	1	2	3	4	5	6	7
Overall, the interview went extremely well.	1	2	3	4	5	6	7

How would you describe Applicant #2?	*weak*						*strong*
Communications ability	1	2	3	4	5	6	7
Future potential	1	2	3	4	5	6	7
Personal appearance	1	2	3	4	5	6	7
Personality	1	2	3	4	5	6	7
Future ambitions	1	2	3	4	5	6	7
Maturity	1	2	3	4	5	6	7
Relevant work experience	1	2	3	4	5	6	7
Knowledge about company	1	2	3	4	5	6	7

How did the interview with Applicant #2 go?	*disagree*						*agree*
Applicant was able and willing to answer any questions.	1	2	3	4	5	6	7
Applicant tried hard to show interest in the job.	1	2	3	4	5	6	7
Overall, the interview went extremely well.	1	2	3	4	5	6	7

CONSULTING ANALYST WANTED

APPLICANT ASSESSMENT SHEET

How do you think Recruiter #1 would describe you?	weak						strong
Communications ability	1	2	3	4	5	6	7
Future potential	1	2	3	4	5	6	7
Personal appearance	1	2	3	4	5	6	7
Personality	1	2	3	4	5	6	7
Future ambitions	1	2	3	4	5	6	7
Maturity	1	2	3	4	5	6	7
Relevant work experience	1	2	3	4	5	6	7
Knowledge about company	1	2	3	4	5	6	7

How did the interview with Recruiter #1 go?	disagree						agree
Interviewer was able and willing to answer any questions.	1	2	3	4	5	6	7
Interviewer tried hard to recruit me for the job.	1	2	3	4	5	6	7
Overall, the interview went extremely well.	1	2	3	4	5	6	7

How do you think Recruiter #2 would describe you?	weak						strong
Communications ability	1	2	3	4	5	6	7
Future potential	1	2	3	4	5	6	7
Personal appearance	1	2	3	4	5	6	7
Personality	1	2	3	4	5	6	7
Future ambitions	1	2	3	4	5	6	7
Maturity	1	2	3	4	5	6	7
Relevant work experience	1	2	3	4	5	6	7
Knowledge about company	1	2	3	4	5	6	7

How did the interview with Recruiter #2 go?	disagree						agree
Interviewer was able and willing to answer any questions.	1	2	3	4	5	6	7
Interviewer tried hard to recruit me for the job.	1	2	3	4	5	6	7
Overall, the interview went extremely well.	1	2	3	4	5	6	7

8

Who Gets Hired?

Purpose:	1. To examine the criteria used by review panels to make decisions about candidates for a managerial position.
	2. To examine the dynamics of conducting interviews and making hiring decisions that occur in review panels.
	3. To examine how treatment and outcome discrimination may be manifested by review panels in the interview process.
Preparation:	Read background sheet
Time:	60 to 75 minutes

BACKGROUND

The introduction to the previous learning activity, Consulting Analyst Wanted, applies to this one as well, except that review panels conduct interviews of two candidates playing specific roles. As a result, we see whether interviews conducted by a review panel rather than a single individual result in treatment discrimination (how interviews are conducted) or outcome discrimination (who gets hired and at what salary).

AUTHOR'S NOTE: This exercise was prepared by L. V. Entrekin and G. N. Soutar. It is from Entrekin, L. V., & Soutar, G. N. (1977). Who gets hired? A male/female role play. In J. W. Pfeiffer & J. E. Jones (Eds.), *A handbook of structured experiences for human relations training*, vol. VI. San Diego, CA: University Associates.

PROCEDURE

1. In a prior class, the instructor will designate two participants to play the roles of Harold Jones and Janet Oliver, the individuals to be interviewed.

2. The instructor will select 10 participants to serve on two five-person review panels that will interview Harold and Janet. Review panels will be given a salary range for the open position. All other participants will act as silent observers, focusing on either Review Panel 1's two interviews, Review Panel 2's two interviews, Harold's two interviews, or Janet's two interviews. (10 minutes)

3. Review the Background Sheet and prepare for the interviews. Review panels should be in separate rooms if possible. Observers with a similar focus (review panels or applicants) should convene to discuss what to look for in interviews. (5 minutes)

4. *First round of interviews*: Review Panel 1 interviews Harold and Review Panel 2 interviews Janet. (15 minutes)

5. Review panel members record their impressions of the candidate on the Review Panel Evaluation Sheet. Observers record their impressions of the interview on the Observer's Worksheet. (5 minutes)

6. *Second round of interviews*: Review Panel 1 interviews Janet and Review Panel 2 interviews Harold. (15 minutes)

7. Each review panel decides (a) which of the two candidates to hire for the job and (b) what salary to offer the candidate, taking into account the salary range for the position. During this time, observers record and share their perceptions with each other, and Janet and Harold meet to compare treatments by the review panels. (5 minutes)

8. Each review panel announces its hiring and salary decisions and underlying rationale. (5 minutes)

9. Participate in a discussion based on the following questions: (remaining time)
   a. How was positive versus negative information about applicants used by the review panels?

b. How did the two review panels differ in their general treatment of applicants?

c. Was there any evidence of treatment discrimination in how the two candidates were treated by the review panels during interviews?

d. Was there any evidence of outcome discrimination in the hiring and salary decisions made by the review panels?

e. What are appropriate criteria to use in making such decisions? Inappropriate criteria?

WHO GETS HIRED?

BACKGROUND SHEET

A large hospital is looking for a manager to oversee its records department, consisting of 15 female employees and an administrative assistant. The records department is responsible for filing patients' records and providing them to authorized hospital staff. It performs a critical function, as the hospital must maintain the security and privacy of patient records in compliance with strict government regulations.

It is hospital policy to promote from within whenever possible. Jim Baker, the manager for the past two years, is being promoted, thereby creating the vacancy. He came into the position with a community college background. Two employees, Janet Oliver and Harold Jones, have applied for the position. Each knows about the other's application.

Janet Oliver is currently the administrative assistant for Jim Baker. She is 43 and has been in the department for 15 years, ten as a records clerk and five in her present position. She is thoroughly familiar with the requirements of the department and is considered an excellent performer. Her tendency to refer to her vast experience in the department, however, and her sometimes abrasive, superior attitude can make people uncomfortable.

Janet first applied for the position at the time Jim Baker was hired. She was told that he was selected over her because of his superior background. Since then, she has obtained an associate degree in human resource management at the local community college and has taken courses on enhancing managerial skills. Janet has told her friends that if she does not get the job this time, she will probably file a discrimination complaint with the regional office of the Equal Employment Opportunity Commission. She has no ambitions to rise above this job in the hospital's management ranks. She is a single parent of a teenage daughter who will graduate from high school next year and hopes to enter college.

Harold Jones is 23 and has a bachelor's degree in health care management from the state university. He has worked in the hospital's Accounting Department for 18 months and has obtained a thorough understanding of hospital operations. Although Harold has been an excellent performer in his position and is considered to have outstanding managerial potential, some people see him as too slick and others as too naive.

Harold views the position of Manager of Hospital Records as a significant step that will allow him to demonstrate his potential for top-level positions. Thus, he does not anticipate spending more than two or three years in this position before moving up in the management ranks. He is married and the father of one preschool son.

WHO GETS HIRED?

REVIEW PANEL EVALUATION SHEET

1. General impressions of your interview with Harold:

2. General impressions of your interview with Janet:

3. Which candidate do you believe is more qualified? Why?

WHO GETS HIRED?

OBSERVER'S WORKSHEET

1. Candidate observed: _____   Review Panel observed: _____

   General impressions of the interview:

2. Candidate observed: _____   Review Panel observed: _____

   General impressions of the interview:

3. What differences did you see in how the two interviews were conducted?

9

The Prison "Break"

Purpose:	1. To examine the challenges faced by former prisoners in gaining employment.
	2. To explore group dynamics during a decision-making task.
	3. To identify individual behaviors that contribute to group effectiveness.
	4. To consider the influence of dimensions of diversity on group behavior.
Preparation:	Complete questionnaire
Time:	60 to 75 minutes

BACKGROUND

Most employers screen potential job candidates with background searches, credit reports, drug testing, and other tools. These practices make it difficult for ex-convicts to re-enter the workforce. Employers see that an applicant spent time in prison and may assume that the candidate possesses undesirable traits—little job experience, lack of skills, drug or alcohol abuse, etc. The odds of released inmates who are unable to successfully re-enter into society being re-incarcerated are overwhelming. Improving these odds is not only in the inmates' best interests but also that of society in general. Research shows that employers are not averse to employing former prisoners, as long as the circumstances are right. The challenge is to create successful employment situations for both the employer and the employee. This

AUTHOR'S NOTE: This exercise was prepared by Vanessa I. Cabral, Gregory W. Fearn, Jennifer Griffin, Jennifer Lenk, Stephanie J. Olender, and Gary N. Powell.

exercise asks a hiring panel to decide among several candidates with criminal records who have applied for a particular job.

As they work on decision-making tasks like this one, members of a group may exhibit different types of behavior. **Task behavior**, which attempts to solve a problem, is exhibited by group members who initiate discussion, offer relevant information or opinions, consider information and opinions offered by others, pull together related ideas, and try to reach consensus on a possible solution. **Social behavior**, which promotes positive interpersonal relations, is exhibited when group members attempt to reconcile disagreements, use humor to reduce group tensions, make sure that everyone has a chance to be heard, encourage others to express ideas, and recognize group process issues that need to be resolved. In most situations, both types of behavior are necessary for a group to be effective, with the former moving the group closer to completion of its task and the latter preserving group harmony.

Thus, the purpose of this exercise is to examine both (1) the challenges faced by former prisoners in gaining employment and (2) the dynamics that occur when groups strive to reach consensus on an important decision.

PROCEDURE

1. Prior to class, complete the questionnaire by assigning your personal rankings to the five candidates for the job.

2. Form groups of five to seven members.

3. As a group, reach a decision on the rankings of all applicants. (30 minutes)

4. Complete the worksheet as a group. (15 minutes)

5. Participate in a discussion based on the following questions: (remaining time)

   a. Questions about the hiring decision:

      (1) How did each group rank the candidates?

      (2) Which experiences, skills, and qualifications were most relevant to this hiring decision?

      (3) How did the candidates' criminal backgrounds influence the hiring decision?

(4) What challenges do former prisoners face in gaining employment?

(5) What can companies and managers do to create successful employment opportunities for former prisoners?

b. Questions about group decision making:

(1) What kinds of task and social behaviors were exhibited during this exercise?

(2) Did any group members specialize in task or social behavior?

(3) Which group member was the most influential? Least influential? Emerged as the group's leader(s)?

(4) What other noteworthy differences in behavior were present?

(5) Were there any differences in behavior according to dimensions of diversity such as sex, race, ethnicity, age, or some other personal characteristic?

REFERENCE   Powell, G. N. (2011). Chapter 5, Working in diverse teams. *Women and men in management*, 4th ed. (pp. 103–125). Thousand Oaks, CA: Sage.

THE PRISON "BREAK"

QUESTIONNAIRE

A major metropolitan newspaper has been asked to participate in a state-run rehabilitation program for released prisoners to assist them in finding employment. If it chooses to participate in the program, it can benefit from special state tax incentives of up to $2400 per qualified individual hired through the program. As part of its corporate responsibility, the newspaper has decided to fill one of three open positions in its circulation department in accordance with the guidelines of the state program. It is currently looking for a Circulation Coordinator to assist circulation management in planning, organizing, and reporting on all sales, customer service, and strategic initiatives. Your group will make the hiring decision.

Responsibilities for this position include the following:

1. Completing daily, weekly, monthly, and quarterly reports for customer service and consumer marketing teams.

2. Updating management reporting books on a monthly and quarterly basis.

3. Processing weekly payroll for telemarketing and retention team.

4. Performing clerical duties to support call center and consumer marketing areas.

5. Additional departmental support as needed.

Minimum qualifications for the position are the following:

1. A high school diploma.

2. A self-directed, motivated, independent thinker.

3. Strong organizational skills.

4. Willingness to work flexible hours as needed.

5. Proficiency in Excel, Microsoft Word, and email.

6. At least two years of secretarial/administrative experience preferred, but not required.

The candidates for the position are the following:

A. Margaret Jones. *Criminal record*: Vehicular manslaughter, released 2 weeks ago. *Education*: Received a General Equivalency Diploma (GED), certifying that she has high school–level academic skills, during incarceration with an emphasis on workforce preparation. *Work experience*: Three consecutive summers as a McDonald's drive-through clerk—duties included greeting customers, entering orders into a computer, and being a cashier. Spent sophomore and junior academic years working in the school library during study halls and after school—duties included assisting students in finding books, re-shelving books, answering telephone, and maintaining fax and computer supplies. *Skills*: Fax machine, Word (intermediate), Excel (intermediate), Outlook (expert), Internet searches, copier, multi-line phone, bookkeeping (beginner).

B. Randy Smith. *Criminal record*: Possession of drugs with intent to sell, released one year ago. *Education*: Holds a high school diploma with classes in accounting, business writing, and computer basics. *Work experience*: Three years working at an electronics retailer, one year as an audio equipment installer, two as a sales clerk in car audio department, six months as a telemarketer for car enthusiast magazine, three months as a gas station attendant. *Skills*: Fax machine, Word (beginner/intermediate), Excel (beginner/ intermediate), Outlook (intermediate), copier, multi-line phone, auto repair and product installation (expert), sales, customer service.

C. Jose Rodriguez. *Criminal record*: Driving while intoxicated, third offense, released 6 months ago. *Education*: Holds a high school diploma and has completed three classes at local community college since release. *Work experience*: Two years as clerk working in the seafood department of a large supermarket, 2 ½ years working at another supermarket in the produce department and as a cashier, four-month temporary assignment as front desk receptionist for a business park. *Skills*: Cash register, Word (beginner), Excel (beginner), Outlook (beginner), fax and copier. *Schedule constraints*: unable to work Tuesday and Thursday before noon due to community college classes.

D. Tu Ying Choi. *Criminal record*: Soliciting a prostitute, second offense, released 10 months ago. *Education*: Earned GED, received certificates of completion for online seminars in Writing and Grammar for Business, Communicating with Tact and Finesse, and Microsoft Beginner Basics. *Work experience*: Four years as a clerk and cashier in a family-owned store, seasonal work at local nursery as cashier and stock clerk over two years, two-month temporary assignment at doctor's office as an after-hours call service representative, nine-month temporary assignment in mailroom and as a file clerk for a large delivery company. *Skills*: Cashier, customer service, mail sorter, fax machine, multi-line phone, Word (intermediate), Excel (beginner), Outlook (intermediate), copier, bookkeeping (beginner).

E. Tanisha Roberts. *Criminal record*: Receiving stolen property and illegal use of prescriptions, released 2 weeks ago. *Education*: Holds high school diploma, was a member of VICA (Vocational Industrial Clubs of America). *Work experience*: Two years as a high-school student volunteer at a large hospital—duties included providing information and service to families; and working in clerical or office capacities as needed. One year as a sales clerk at a discount clothier; duties included stocking floor, monitoring dressing rooms, assisting customers, and cashier as needed. *Skills*: Computerized cash register, customer service, filing, some basic medical coding, multi-line phone, copier, fax, Word (intermediate), Excel (beginner), Outlook (intermediate).

Before your group meets, rank order your *personal* choices for who should get the job and record your choices in the table below (first choice "1," second choice "2," and so on).

Your group needs to reach a decision on the rankings of *all* candidates by *consensus*; it cannot vote. Reaching a decision by consensus does not mean that every member thinks that the best decision has been made, but that all members consent to it and no members strongly object. If no consensus can be reached, the position will go unfilled and the job search terminated. Record your group's rankings in the table below.

Candidate	*Your Personal Rankings*	*Your Group's Rankings*
A. Margaret Jones		
B. Randy Smith		
C. Jose Rodriguez		
D. Tu Ying Choi		
E. Tanisha Roberts		

THE PRISON "BREAK"

WORKSHEET

1. Which member(s) of your group:

   a. Exhibited *task behaviors* (e.g., initiated discussion, offered relevant information or opinions, considered information and opinions offered by others, pulled together related ideas, tried to reach consensus on a possible solution)?

   b. Exhibited *social behaviors* (e.g., attempted to reconcile disagreements, used humor to reduce group tensions, made sure that everyone had a chance to be heard, encouraged others to express ideas, recognized group process issues that needed to be resolved)?

   c. Spoke the most during the group's discussion? The least?

   d. Was the most influential? Least influential? Emerged as the group's leader(s)?

   e. Interrupted others the most? The least?

2. Were there any differences in behavior according to dimensions of diversity such as sex, race, ethnicity, age, or some other personal characteristic? If so, what were they?

10 Beyond O. J.

Purpose:
1. To examine how members of different races communicate in the workplace.
2. To identify ways to make communication positive and constructive rather than negative and destructive for race relations in the workplace.
3. To use national and world events as tools for improving workplace relationships among members of different races.

Preparation: None

Time: 60 to 75 minutes

BACKGROUND

On October 3, 1995, a "not guilty" verdict was announced in the murder trial of O. J. Simpson. Simpson, a Black man and popular ex-football player, sports announcer, and actor, had been charged with the murders of Nicole Brown Simpson, his White ex-wife, and Ronald Goldman, her White friend. Reactions were immediate and intense. A hopeful diversity consultant predicted that the gulf in Black-White relations "will wake people up at work." However, the verdict was generally characterized as representing a negative milestone for race

AUTHOR'S NOTE: This exercise was prepared by Gary N. Powell and Kevin B. Taylor. It is reprinted with permission from Powell, G. N., and Taylor, K. B. (1998). Beyond O.J.: Examining race relations in the workplace. *Journal of Management Education: A Publication of the OBTS Teaching Society for Management Educators, 22,* 208–217. Copyright © The Organizational Behavior Teaching Society. Published by SAGE Publications, Inc., on behalf of The Organizational Behavior Teaching Society.

relations in the workplace. One corporate spokesperson reported that an "intellectual riot" broke out as Black and White employees debated the issue. A despondent observer concluded:

> where once (Simpson) was the quintessential example of how a Black person could successfully transcend race, now he is the quintessential excuse for why Blacks and Whites will, for the most part, remain separate. . . . We know exactly how to heal our racial divide: by getting to know each other as *individuals*. Unfortunately, now that possibility seems more remote than at any other time in the past 20 years.

Since then, many other incidents have focused attention on race relations in society. For example, when he was a candidate in the 2008 U.S. presidential election, Barack Obama was the target of racist comments about his Muslim-sounding middle name, Hussein; Obama is of mixed race but identified himself as Black on a census form. Shortly after Obama was elected president, Harvard scholar Henry Louis Gates Jr., who is Black, was arrested outside his Cambridge, Massachusetts, home after a neighbor reported seeing two Black men in the predominantly White neighborhood trying to force open the door; Gates had locked himself outside of his own home. President Obama hosted Gates and the White arresting officer, Sergeant James Crowley of the Cambridge Police Department, for beers at the White House afterwards in an attempt to defuse the incident. Also, MSNBC television host Chris Matthews came under fire for saying that Obama had done so much to heal racial divides that "I forgot he was Black" after Obama's first State of the Union address. The controversy over Matthews's comment suggested that racial divides, at least in U.S. society, had not yet been healed.

This exercise was developed to examine what happens when coworkers of different races converse about a race-related incident. Since public events that focus attention on racial divisions in society occur often, the purpose of this exercise is to use the public event of the moment as a vehicle to consider ways to promote positive race relations in the workplace.

PROCEDURE

1. In a prior class, the instructor will select two volunteers of different races to prepare and perform a skit that will focus on a recent race-related incident.

2. Observe the skit. (15 to 20 minutes)

3. Participate in a discussion based on the following questions: (remaining time)

   a. What happened in each of the three meetings depicted in the skit?

   b. Which meeting best depicted how coworkers of different races would truthfully communicate about a race-related incident?

   c. Which meeting best depicted how coworkers of different races might actually interact concerning a race-related incident?

   d. What would it take for members of different races in the workplace to have discussions of issues that resemble the third meeting in the skit?

   e. Is it appropriate to use work time to discuss race-related incidents that involve others and take place outside of work?

REFERENCES

Cooper, H., & Goodnough, A. (2009, July 31). Over beers, no apologies, but plans to have lunch. *New York Times*. Retrieved July 31, 2009, from http://www.nytimes.com.

"I forgot he was Black": Chris Matthews under fire for comment about Obama. (2010, January 28). *Fox News*. Retrieved February 4, 2010, from http://www.foxnews.com.

Pearson, H. (1995, October 11). After O. J.: Racial divide simply grows. *Wall Street Journal*, A14.

Roberts, S., & Baker, P. (2010, April 2). Asked to declare his race, Obama checks "Black." *New York Times*. Retrieved April 3, 2010, from http://www.nytimes.com.

Simpson verdict is seen as milestone for workplace race relations. (1995, October 10). *Wall Street Journal*, A1.

11 Designer Decorations

Purpose:	To examine behaviors that contribute to leader effectiveness in

      a. Directing a team of subordinates working on a task.

      b. Representing a group competing for scarce organizational resources.

      c. Making decisions about how to allocate scarce organizational resources.

      d. Serving as a role model and inspirational force for the entire organization.

Preparation:	Bring old newspapers, magazines, and art supplies to the class
Time:	2 to 2½ hours over one or two class sessions

BACKGROUND

Managers or **leaders** (the terms are used interchangeably) influence the actions of their subordinates through the leadership style they adopt. Leadership style may be characterized in several ways. **Task style**, which focuses on task accomplishment, refers to the extent to which the manager initiates and organizes work activity and defines the way work is to be done. For example, a manager who reorganizes a department, develops a description of the function of each department member, formulates department and individual goals, assigns projects, and gives details on how projects should be conducted may

---

AUTHOR'S NOTE: This exercise was prepared by Gary N. Powell.

be considered high in task style. **Interpersonal style**, which focuses on maintenance of interpersonal relationships, refers to the extent to which the manager engages in activities that tend to the morale and welfare of people. For example, a manager who expresses appreciation to subordinates for work performed well, demonstrates concern about their job and work satisfaction, and tries to build their self-esteem may be considered high in interpersonal style. A manager may be high in both task and interpersonal style, low in both, or high in one but not the other.

Managers may also exhibit different decision-making styles. A leader who exhibits a **democratic style of decision making** allows subordinates to participate in decision making, whereas a leader who exhibits an **autocratic style of decision making** discourages such participation.

In addition, a distinction may be made between transformational and transactional leadership. **Transformational leaders** motivate subordinates to transcend their own self-interests for the good of the group or organization by setting exceptionally high standards for performance and then developing subordinates to achieve these standards. In this way, they turn followers into leaders. Transformational leaders exhibit four types of behavior: (a) *charisma*, by displaying attributes that induce followers to view them as role models and behaviors that communicate a sense of values, purpose, and the importance of the mission; (b) *inspirational motivation*, by exuding optimism and excitement about the mission and its attainability; (c) *intellectual stimulation*, by encouraging followers to question basic assumptions and consider problems and tasks from new perspectives; and (d) *individualized consideration*, by focusing on the development and mentoring of followers as individuals and attending to their specific needs.

In contrast, **transactional leaders** focus on clarifying the responsibilities of subordinates and then responding to how well subordinates execute their responsibilities. They exhibit two kinds of behavior: (a) *contingent reward*, by promising and providing suitable rewards if followers achieve their assigned objectives, and (b) *management by exception*, by intervening to correct follower performance either in anticipation of a problem or after a problem has occurred. Transactional leaders who engage in active management by exception systematically monitor subordinate performance for mistakes, whereas those who engage in passive management by exception wait for subordinate difficulties to be brought to their attention before intervening. Transformational leaders may be transactional when it is necessary to achieve their goals. However, transactional leaders are seldom transformational.

Distinct from both transformational and transactional leadership is **laissez-faire leadership**. Laissez-faire leaders avoid taking responsibility for leadership altogether. Such leaders refrain from giving direction or making decisions and do not involve themselves in the development of their followers.

The purpose of this exercise is to examine how these types of leader behavior apply to a variety of critical roles that leaders play in organizations.

PROCEDURE

1. Bring old magazines, newspapers, and art supplies to the class.

2. The instructor will assign four-to-six person teams and will designate one person as team leader and one as company president. Each team is to respond to the following directive, to be read by the company president (10 minutes):

> Our company, Designer Decorations, makes "designer products" that enhance the ambiance of a living or work area. These products may represent a concrete image (e.g., a well-known building or monument) or something more abstract.
>
> Your project team has been asked to submit a proposal for a new product. Because we can bring only one new product to market at this time, only one design will be chosen. You will be competing with other teams to have your design selected. The primary criteria for selection are conceptual appeal and attractiveness; cost is a secondary consideration for now. Although a higher price for a high-status designer label such as ours may actually stimulate sales, there is a limit as to how much potential customers will pay.
>
> Each team will have 60 minutes to decide on a design and build a prototype of it from the materials available that I can inspect and evaluate, though the final product may be built from different materials. Following the planning and building period, I will hold a staff meeting with team leaders to review the designs and decide which, if any, will be selected. The team whose prototype is selected will design the finished product. Other teams will be disbanded and their members reassigned.

3. As a team, plan the design of your product and build a prototype. (60 minutes)

4. Complete Part A of the Questionnaire. (5 minutes)

5. In the meeting with the company president, each team leader will present and defend the design of his or her group. At the end of the meeting or shortly thereafter, the president will decide which design, if any, will be adopted and will then communicate this decision. Project team members may observe the staff meeting but must remain silent. (30 minutes)

6. Complete Part B of the Questionnaire. (5 minutes)

7. Participate in a discussion based on the following questions: (remaining time)

    a. How well did the project team leaders direct their teams' planning and building effort? What leadership style did they exhibit? What leader behaviors were most effective? Least effective?

    b. How well did the project team leaders represent their respective teams in the president's staff meeting? What leader behaviors were most effective in influencing the decision about which design to choose? Least effective?

    c. How effective was the president as a leader? Was the president high or low in task style and interpersonal style? Did the president exhibit an autocratic or democratic decision-making style in running the staff meeting? Was the president a transformational, transactional, or laissez-faire leader?

d. Did the "best" design win the competition? Why or why not?

e. How did the fact that the specified criteria for design selection were entirely subjective influence behavior?

f. What examples did you see of effective *follower* behaviors?

g. How did dimensions of diversity influence the results of the exercise?

REFERENCE   Powell, G. N. (2011). Chapter 6, Leading people. *Women and men in management*, 4th ed. (pp. 126–150). Thousand Oaks, CA: Sage.

DESIGNER DECORATIONS

QUESTIONNAIRE

Instructions: Use a 1 to 5 scale for all questions except #8, with 1 as low and 5 as high.

PART A: COMPLETE BEFORE THE STAFF MEETING

_____   1. How satisfied are you with how your team functioned?

_____   2. How satisfied are you with the role you played in your team's task?

_____   3. How do you evaluate the merits of your team's design?

_____   4. How do you rate your leader in task style?

_____   5. How do you rate your leader in interpersonal style?

_____   6. How satisfied are you with your leader's performance so far?

PART B: COMPLETE AFTER THE STAFF MEETING

_____   7. How satisfied are you with how your leader represented your team in the staff meeting?

_____   8. Did the president use a democratic or autocratic decision-making style in the staff meeting?

_____   9. How do you rate the president as a transformational leader?

_____ 10. How do you rate the president as a transactional leader?

_____ 11. How satisfied are you with the president's overall performance?

_____ 12. How confident are you that the design chosen is in the company's best interest?

12 Dealing With Sexually Oriented Behavior

Purpose: 1. To examine personal reactions to workplace situations with sexual overtones.
              2. To examine personal and legal definitions of sexual harassment.

Preparation: Complete questionnaire

Time: 60 to 75 minutes

BACKGROUND

Sexual harassment occurs when one individual directs unwelcome sexual attention toward another. In recent years, incidents involving a U.S. president, a Supreme Court nominee, a senator, military officers, professional athletes, and corporate chief executive officers have received considerable publicity. Although most people recognize that a line needs to be drawn between acceptable and unacceptable sexually oriented behavior in the workplace, the question remains as to exactly what types of behavior constitute sexual harassment. In other words, where should the line be drawn?

Sexual harassment is a pervasive phenomenon. Although the proportion of women who report having experienced sexually

AUTHOR'S NOTE: This exercise was prepared by Gary N. Powell. The vignettes in the questionnaire were adapted from a survey on sexual harassment reported in Collins, E. G. C., & Blodgett, T. B. (1981). Sexual harassment . . . some see it . . . some won't. *Harvard Business Review, 59*(3), 76–95.

harassing behavior at work depends somewhat on the research method used to assess the prevalence of sexual harassment, it is 54% across all types of studies. The proportion of men who have been sexually harassed at work is not as high but still worthy of note. In 2008, over 13,000 sexual harassment complaints were filed with the U.S. Equal Employment Opportunity Commission (EEOC), 16% of which were filed by men.

Sexual harassment is also a cross-cultural phenomenon. Studies have confirmed the prevalence of sexual harassment in many nations, and public consciousness of the issue has spread worldwide. For example, in Japan, public consciousness of sexual harassment, or **sekuhara**, emerged after the nation's first hostile environment court case received considerable media attention. However, norms regarding the acceptability of sexually oriented behavior at work vary across national cultures, with American laws and customs stricter in many cases than those elsewhere.

In the United States, sexual harassment, an unlawful employment practice under Title VII of the Civil Rights Act, is defined as "unwelcome sexual advances, requests for sexual favors, and other verbal or physical conduct of a sexual nature" when submission to or rejection of the conduct enters into employment decisions and/or the conduct interferes with work performance or creates a hostile work environment. Two types of harassment are actionable under Title VII, quid pro quo harassment and hostile environment harassment. In **quid pro quo sexual harassment**, the harasser asks the victim to participate in sexual activity in return for gaining a job, promotion, raise, or other reward. In **hostile environment sexual harassment**, one employee makes sexual requests, comments, looks, and so on toward another employee and thereby creates a hostile work environment. An organization may be held responsible for sexual harassment by its employees when it knew or should have known of the conduct, unless it can show that it took immediate and appropriate corrective action.

Legal definitions are somewhat vague, however, and employers and courts must interpret exactly what constitutes sexual harassment. Given this uncertainty, individuals' own definitions assume considerable importance in determining the sexually oriented behaviors that they feel entitled to initiate and their responses to behaviors initiated by others. The purpose of this exercise is to examine how personal and legal definitions of sexual harassment may be applied to different workplace situations.

PROCEDURE   1. Prior to class, complete the questionnaire that follows.

2. Participate in a discussion based on the following questions:

a. How do you think *most people* would respond in each situation?

b. How would *you* respond in each situation?

c. In which situations did sexual harassment occur according to your own personal definition? According to legal definitions?

d. What can organizations do to try to prevent sexual harassment from occurring?

e. How should organizations deal with incidents of alleged sexual harassment?

REFERENCE   Powell, G. N. (2011). Chapter 7, Dealing with sexuality in the workplace. *Women and men in management*, 4th ed. (pp. 151–179). Thousand Oaks, CA: Sage.

DEALING WITH SEXUALLY ORIENTED BEHAVIOR

QUESTIONNAIRE

1. As president of your company, you walk into the office of the sales manager to congratulate him on setting a new record. When you enter the office, the sales manager is standing very close to his administrative assistant, who looks upset and flustered.

   a. What do you think *most company presidents* would do?

   b. What would *you* do?

   c. Does the sales manager's behavior constitute sexual harassment?

2. You enter an elevator with another middle-management-level executive of the same sex. That person stares at the body of the other occupant of the elevator (a lower-level employee of the opposite sex) for a few seconds, mutters a suggestive remark, and then winks at you. You see that the employee has noticed the attention.

   a. What do you think *most executives* would do?

   b. What would *you* do?

   c. Does the other executive's behavior constitute sexual harassment?

d. How would your responses to these questions differ if the employee had *not* noticed the attention?

3. An assistant vice president (AVP) is one of the most promising executives in your company. He complains to you, the division manager, that his boss has been making unwelcome and persistent sexual advances. You have a private conversation with his boss, who insists that the AVP has mistaken her "innocent" remarks and gestures.

   a. What do you think *most division managers* would do?

   b. What would *you* do?

   c. Does the behavior by the AVP's boss constitute sexual harassment?

4. A junior administrator in a large hospital has been the object of persistent sexual advances from a doctor who works for the medical practice that is one of the primary users of the hospital's facilities. She says she has tried to discourage these advances tactfully, some of which have occurred in the presence of her coworkers, but has been unsuccessful. The woman complains to you, the chief hospital administrator.

   a. What do you think *most chief administrators* would do?

   b. What would *you* do?

   c. Does the doctor's behavior constitute sexual harassment?

13

Mixing Sex and Work

Purpose: 1. To identify a range of personal, ethical, professional, and organizational considerations related to workplace romances.
2. To examine the effects of such relationships on individual as well as organizational effectiveness.

Preparation: None

Time: 60 to 75 minutes

BACKGROUND

Sexual interest in a coworker is not always unwelcome. In some cases, it is reciprocated and serves as the basis for a relationship between two employees that goes beyond their work roles. **Workplace romance,** or a mutually-desired relationship between two people at work in which some element of sexuality or physical intimacy exists, has become more prevalent in recent years due to fundamental changes in the workplace. Individuals have greater opportunity to become romantically involved with an organizational member of the opposite sex due to the increased proportion of women in the labor force, especially in managerial and professional jobs. Also, employees are expected to work longer hours, leading to their spending more

AUTHOR'S NOTE: This exercise was prepared by Peggy Morrison. It is from Morrison, P. (1979). Sexual values in organizations: An OD role play. In J. W. Pfeiffer & J. E. Jones (Eds.), *A handbook of structured experiences for human relations training*, vol. VII. San Diego, CA: University Associates.

time with coworkers and less time with family members. As a result, the work environment has become increasingly conducive to the formation of romantic relationships. About 40% of workers say that they have dated a coworker at some point in their careers.

Although most people like to believe in happy endings, workplace romances can be controversial. Catharine MacKinnon, one of the first scholars of sexual harassment, argued that most of what passes for workplace romance is actually sexual harassment in disguise, resulting from a patriarchal system in which women are powerless to avoid being exploited sexually. Margaret Mead, a famed anthropologist, argued that, much like taboos against sexual expression in the family that are necessary for children to grow up safely, taboos against sexual involvement at work are necessary for men and women to work together effectively. However, others claim that it is foolish to try to regulate welcome sexual attention. As one manager put it, "Trying to outlaw romance is like trying to outlaw the weather."

Most individuals need both intimacy and accomplishment. Because the workplace is a convenient setting for meeting others, individuals frequently have to choose which need, if not both, they will fulfill. While recognizing that romantic relationships pose problems for their organizations, people's own needs may conflict, and must be reconciled, with the needs of the business. The purpose of this exercise is to consider how workplace romances may influence the conduct of work and what management should do about them, if anything.

PROCEDURE

1. In a prior class, the instructor will select at least five volunteers to prepare a skit for class presentation.

2. Observe the skit. (15 minutes)

3. Participate in a discussion based on the following questions: (remaining time)

   a. What were your personal reactions to the skit?

   b. How did the relationship influence the effectiveness of:

      (1) the individuals involved?

      (2) coworkers?

      (3) the organization as a whole?

c. What would you do if you were the *manager* of either or both partners and you discovered the romantic relationship:

      (1) while it was going on?

      (2) after it ended?

d. What would you do if you were a *coworker* of either or both partners?

e. Have you had any personal experiences related to issues raised by the skit, either as a participant or an observer?

REFERENCES

Hymowitz, C., & Pollock, E. J. (1998, February 4). Corporate affairs: The one clear line in interoffice romance has become blurred. *Wall Street Journal*, p. A1.

MacKinnon, C. A. (1979). *Sexual harassment of working women: A case of sex discrimination.* New Haven, CT: Yale University Press.

Mead, M. (1980). A proposal: We need taboos on sex at work. In D. A. Neugarten and J. M. Shafritz (Eds.), *Sexuality in organizations: Romantic and coercive behaviors at work* (pp. 53–56). Oak Park, IL: Moore.

Parks, M. (2006). *2006 workplace romance: Poll findings.* Alexandria, VA: Society for Human Resource Management. Retrieved October 26, 2009, from http://www.shrm.org.

Powell, G. N. (2011). Chapter 7, Dealing with sexuality in the workplace. *Women and men in management*, 4th ed. (pp. 151–179). Thousand Oaks, CA: Sage.

14

Have I Got
Good News for Us!

Purpose:	1. To examine issues faced by dual-career couples when relocation is involved.
	2. To examine the influence of children on relocation decisions.
Preparation:	None
Time:	60 to 75 minutes

BACKGROUND

Relocation to a different region of the same country or a different country enhances employees' development and likelihood of future career success by providing them the chance to polish their skills, work on high-visibility projects, and gain valuable first-hand perspective on the problems and challenges faced in different corporate facilities. Because global business has become a major component of most corporations' operations, international assignments are particularly valuable opportunities for upwardly mobile managers.

Married women are offered fewer job opportunities requiring relocation, including international assignments, than married men. Organizational decision makers tend to assume that women will be less willing to accept relocation offers than men because such a stance is less disruptive to their families. In reality, women do not express less of a willingness to relocate domestically or accept international assignments than men. However, because they are perceived to be

AUTHOR'S NOTE: This exercise was prepared by Jeffrey H. Greenhaus. © Jeffrey H. Greenhaus. Used with permission.

less willing to move their families, women experience lower geographic mobility than men, which restricts their career success.

Employees do differ, though, in their willingness to relocate for a new job with the same employer. Overall, married employees of both sexes who are younger, more ambitious, and have more supportive spouses are more willing to relocate.

The spouse may have the most difficult role of any family member in a relocation. Whereas the employee remains in the same organization and children have the routine of school, spouses often leave behind work, friends, and other family members without having any structure or continuity to support them. The spouse's dissatisfaction is the most frequently reported reason for an employee's unsuccessful relocation. In the case of temporary international assignments, the spouse's inability or unwillingness to adapt may require the family to come home early and the employee to terminate the assignment prematurely.

When employees consider whether to accept a job opportunity that requires relocation, they must balance the desire to enhance their future career success and the desire to have a healthy and happy family life. The purpose of this exercise is to examine how employees and family members react when these two concerns conflict and how employers can help employees resolve such conflicts.

PROCEDURE

1. Form groups of three members. Decide who will play the role of the mother (Lisa Sanders), the father (Dave Sanders), and the teenage son or daughter (Steve or Stephanie Sanders). Review the role description provided by the instructor and prepare to play your role. (10 minutes)

2. After the instructor announces that dinner is served, Dave, Lisa, and Steve/Stephanie begin their evening meal, with Lisa serving the take-out food she bought on the way home. Family dinners are usually done in 20–30 minutes. (20 to 30 minutes)

3. Participate in a discussion based on the following questions: (remaining time)

   a. What was the outcome of the dinnertime discussion?

   b. How was work-family conflict exhibited?

    c. Were family members supportive of each other?

    d. How would you describe the decision-making process used?

    e. Which family member had the most influence over the final outcome?

    f. To what extent was each family member satisfied with the outcome?

    g. What can organizations do to help their employees deal with such situations?

REFERENCES

Adler, N. J. (1984). Women do not want international careers: And other myths about international management. *Organizational Dynamics, 13*(2), 66–79.

Brett, J. M., Stroh, L. K., & Reilly, A. H. (1993). Pulling up roots in the 1990s: Who's willing to relocate? *Journal of Organizational Behavior, 14,* 49–60.

Lyness, K. S., & Thompson, D. E. (2000). Climbing the corporate ladder: Do female and male executives follow the same route? *Journal of Applied Psychology, 85,* 86–101.

Powell, G. N. (2011). Chapter 8, Managing the work-family interface. *Women and men in management*, 4th ed. (pp. 180–212). Thousand Oaks, CA: Sage.

Stroh, L. K., Brett, J. M., & Reilly, A. H. (1992). All the right stuff: A comparison of female and male managers' career progression. *Journal of Applied Psychology, 77,* 251–260.

15

Managing From a Distance

Purpose:	1. To explore the benefits, costs, and challenges of telecommuting to both employees and employers.
	2. To examine how biases may influence management decisions relating to telecommuting.
	3. To explore the challenges faced by management in deciding which employees will be granted the opportunity to telecommute.
Preparation:	Complete the questionnaire
Time:	60 to 75 minutes

BACKGROUND

Telecommuting, being paid to do some or all of one's work away from the work site, is an increasingly popular type of work arrangement as more work becomes virtual. Telecommuting is most common for managerial and professional employees. It gives employees flexibility in the location and timing of work by allowing them to work out of a virtual office. Telecommuters report that working at home increases their productivity by reducing work interruptions and distractions and enhancing their concentration. It also helps employees to balance work and family; their increased presence at home enables them to better fulfill their childcare and household responsibilities and strengthens family relationships.

AUTHOR'S NOTE: This exercise was prepared by Jeannine DePhillips, Tricia A. Hyacinth, Rasha D. Jones-Warren, Cora E. LaFrance, Martha Reed Ossias, Kristen M. Schuliar, and Gary N. Powell.

However, telecommuters may feel disconnected from colleagues and have fewer advancement opportunities than employees who work in the office and have more "face time" with supervisors. Telecommuting can also blur the boundary between work and family roles in unproductive ways. Because work-related messages arrive electronically around the clock, telecommuters may feel pressured to work around the clock. Telecommuters also face interruptions and distractions (children, pets, television, household chores, and so on) from being at home. As a result, telecommuting may both decrease the extent to which work interferes with family and increase the extent to which family interferes with work. It presents unique challenges to employees that they would not face if they had a more traditional work arrangement.

Overall, the net effects of telecommuting may be either positive or negative, depending on the situation and the employee. The success of a telecommuting arrangement depends on a combination of an employee's work responsibilities, home responsibilities, and his or her skills and personality. The purpose of this exercise is to examine employers' decisions about which employees will be granted the opportunity to telecommute.

PROCEDURE

1. Prior to class, read the descriptions of employees who are applying for telecommuting assignments. Decide which two applications you would approve.

2. In class, form groups of 5 to 7 members. (5 minutes)

3. As a group, reach a decision as to which two employees will have their telecommuting applications approved. (30 minutes)

4. Participate in a discussion based on the following questions: (remaining time)

   a. Which two telecommuting applications did your group decide to approve?

   b. What criteria were used to determine which applications would be approved?

c. How was work-related versus personal information about applicants used in the decision process?

d. What further information about applicants would you have liked to have as a decision maker?

e. Do you have any personal experience with telecommuting?

f. What challenges would you face in managing a telecommuting employee?

g. Would you treat telecommuting employees differently than other employees? If so, how?

h. What challenges would you face as an employee in making telecommuting work for you? Is it even a possibility?

i. How can an organization take best advantage of telecommuting?

REFERENCES   Golden, T. D., Veiga, J. F., & Simsek, Z. (2006). Telecommuting's differential
                      impact on work-family conflict: Is there no place like home? *Journal of
                      Applied Psychology, 91,* 1340–1350.
                   Hill, E. J., Ferris, M., & Märtinson, V. (2003). Does it matter where you work?
                      A comparison of how three work venues (traditional office, virtual
                      office, and home office) influence aspects of work and personal/family
                      life. *Journal of Vocational Behavior, 63,* 220–241.
                   Hill, E. J., Miller, B. C., Weiner, S. P., & Colihan, J. (1998). Influences of the vir-
                      tual office on aspects of work and work/life balance. *Personnel
                      Psychology, 51,* 667–683.
                   Powell, G. N. (2011). Chapter 8, Managing the work-family interface.
                      Women and men in management, 4th ed. (pp. 180–212). Thousand Oaks,
                      CA: Sage.

MANAGING FROM A DISTANCE

QUESTIONNAIRE

California Telecom Solutions (CTS) is planning to relocate to a new office space in the Los Angeles area because its current landlord has raised its rent by an unacceptable amount. In an effort to save thousands of dollars per month in rent, the company has decided to relocate to a smaller space that will accommodate fewer people. Hence, CTS is initiating a telecommuting program. The company does not yet have a policy for telecommuting. Management, however, has asked CTS managers to identify and recommend two employees from each department for what will be the pilot telecommuting program. You, the Information Technology (IT) manager, have eight subordinates who have expressed an interest in telecommuting. All of the employees' jobs can be done remotely. During the pilot phase of the program, each candidate will be allowed to work from home three days a week. After a 6-month probationary period, each employee will be reassessed to determine whether he or she can telecommute five days a week or whether the privilege should be revoked.

Job descriptions in the IT department are as follows:

Junior Programmer: Write, test, and maintain detailed instructions, called programs, that computers follow to perform their functions. Conceive, design, and test logical structures for solving simple business problems by computer.

Senior Programmer: Write, test, and maintain detailed instructions, called programs, that computers follow to perform their functions. Conceive, design, and test more advanced logical structures for solving complex business problems by computer (more experience required than for Junior Programmer).

Network Engineer: Design and implement computer networks. Focus on networking devices and infrastructure that connect devices on a network.

Database Administrator: Determine ways to organize and store data. Identify user needs and set up new computer databases.

Performance evaluations for CTS employees are based on the following scale:

Poor	*Satisfactory*	*Good*	*Very Good*	*Excellent*
1	2	3	4	5

Employee Profiles

1. **Barry Edwards**, a 45-year-old male, is a Network Engineer who has two small children, ages 1.5 and 6 months. He has been in a long-term relationship with his gay partner, Steve, for 12 years. Although Steve is a stay-at-home parent, he is overwhelmed because their youngest child is premature and requires special need and around the clock attention. Barry has been with CTS for 5 years and has received annual ratings of *very good* consistently. He has a strong work ethic and lives 18 miles from the office.

2. **Veronica Smith** is a 38-year-old single mother of two children, ages 3 and 5. She has been with CTS for 3 years as a Network Engineer. Her eldest son, Earl, occasionally suffers from bouts of asthma. Although he is currently taking medication for his asthma, Veronica believes that he can have a flare-up at any time and would like to be nearby should it happen again. During her first year on the job, she was written up by her manager for using the office telephone to make personal calls. Since that incident, she has not had any issues with using company property inappropriately. She has consistently scored a rating of *good* on her annual performance. Her roundtrip commute is 100 miles.

3. **Barbara Davis** is a 35-year-old single female who was initially hired by the company as a Database Analyst; however, she was quickly promoted to Database Administrator in a short period of time because of her commitment and dedication to the company. She is considered by her peers to be a "workaholic." She joined CTS straight out of college at the age of 21. She lives 15 miles from work and would like to take advantage of telecommuting because she and a fellow Database Administrator have been in contention for several months. She believes that the only way to be productive is to limit her face-to-face time with her co-worker. She has consistently received a rating of very good over the years.

4. **Jacob McKenzie** is a 29-year-old male who has worked at CTS as a Database Administrator for 6 years. For the past 9 months, he has successfully worked on a special project with very little supervision. Jacob's wife is expecting, and Jacob would like to be able to spend more time at home and less time on the road. He has received ratings that vary from *satisfactory* to *good*. He attributes his satisfactory ratings to a previous manager who was not fond of him. His commute is 85 miles each way.

5. **Karen Wilson** is a 45-year-old Senior Programmer and has been with CTS for 9 years. In general, she has received good reviews over that time. However, during the last few years, a few of her co-workers have complained that she is a little difficult to work with. Karen has two children who are in college, and she recently went through a bitter divorce. She lives 50 miles away from work.

6. **Robert Harris** is a 40-year-old Junior Programmer and has been with CTS for 2 years. He has received satisfactory reviews. Robert lives 20 miles from work and is the primary caregiver for

his father (a widower), who is in his early 80s. Last year, Robert's father suffered a mild stroke and, since that time, has been living in Robert's home.

7. **Tom Smith** is a 34-year-old Junior Programmer who has been with the company for 4 years. He has consistently received excellent reviews over the years. Two years ago, he started an e-commerce software business that is doing quite well. Tom lives 40 miles away from work and has 3 children (twin sons—age 2, and a daughter—age 4). His wife is in sales and travels out of state 60% of the time.

8. **Cynthia Clark** is a 40-year-old Junior Programmer and has been with CTS for 7 years. For the last 2 years, she has received satisfactory reviews. Cynthia lives 50 miles away from work. Three years ago, Cynthia had breast cancer surgery. She is very active in several New York–based breast cancer advocacy organizations and is a board member for one of the organizations.

Your choice for which two employees will be allowed to participate in your department's pilot telecommuting program:

Your group's choice:

16

Networking Role Play

Purpose:	1. To demonstrate how people form connections in an informal setting.
	2. To identify behaviors that facilitate and inhibit the formation of connections.
Preparation:	None
Time:	60 to 75 minutes

BACKGROUND

Much popular writing has emphasized the value of personal networks in searching for and obtaining desirable jobs and in promoting advancement within organizations. In fact, some organizations promote networking among women professionals to counteract the exclusion of women from "old boy" networks. Women and men with more fully developed organizational networks are likely to see their career success enhanced. However, interactions that take place in informal settings may be just as important in influencing how others see us and what our working relationships with them are like. Diverse networks can enhance individuals' social capital. The purpose of this exercise is to examine how informal networks between people are established.

AUTHOR'S NOTE: This exercise was prepared by Joyce M. Girard, Cara L. Herman, Linda M. Salafia, and Gary N. Powell.

PROCEDURE   1. The instructor will form 13-person groups in different areas of the classroom with tables and chairs removed or put to the side. Within each group, each participant will receive a brief "personality profile" to review before the role play begins. If the class size does not lend itself to 13-person groups, some of the roles may be eliminated or combined, or some participants may be designated as observers and receive a copy of all personality profiles. (15 minutes)

2. In the role play, you have just arrived at a cocktail party being held by a professional acquaintance in New York City. Feel free to mingle with other guests, whom you are meeting for the first time. (30 minutes)

3. Participate in a discussion based on the following questions: (remaining time)

    a. What did it feel like to interact with strangers in an informal setting?

    b. Did participants interact freely during the cocktail party?

    c. Were participants eager to help each other when they had the opportunity to do so? Were participants willing to introduce a person in need to an individual who might be able to help him or her?

       d. How strong were the connections established between people by the end of the role play?

       e. What specific behaviors helped or restricted the formation of connections between people?

       f. How do responses to these questions differ between groups?

17

We Are Family

Purpose:	1. To examine conflicts that may occur between family and non-family members in family firms.
	2. To examine issues associated with being a non-family employee in a family firm.
	3. To identify ways to build good working relationships between family and non-family members in family firms.

Preparation:	None

Time:	60 to 75 minutes

BACKGROUND

Family firms are businesses in which the family exercises some degree of control over strategic direction and that are intended to remain in the family. They represent a significant portion of the national and global economy. In the United States, over 90% of all businesses are family-owned; family firms contribute almost half of the gross domestic product, employ over half of the workforce, and create over three-quarters of new jobs. An estimated 40% of the *Fortune 500*, including some of the biggest companies in the global economy (e.g., Wal-Mart), are family firms. At some point in many individuals' careers, they may be employed by a family firm, begin their own business and involve family members in it, and/or have a

AUTHOR'S NOTE: This exercise was prepared by Priscilla M. Cale and Gary N. Powell.

business relationship with a family firm as a supplier, distributor, contractor, client, or be involved in some other capacity.

Non-family members may play important roles in family firms. For example, they may contribute innovative ideas that differ from the types of ideas that the firm has usually adopted, mentor the next generation of family members who will eventually attain top management positions, serve as alter egos to family members in top management, and enable the business to meet its goals for growth, profitability, and overall performance. Family firms that do not take full advantage of the potential contributions of non-family members are likely to fare worse than other firms in their industry, whether family-owned or not, that take better advantage of what all of their employees have to offer.

However, non-family members may feel isolated and vulnerable in a family-dominated firm. Non-family members in the managerial ranks may legitimately feel that a "glass ceiling" prevents their advancement to the top of the organization. In addition, they may feel that their views and interests are downplayed compared with the views and interests of family members in equivalent positions. The purpose of this exercise is to explore the intra-firm dynamics that arise between family members and non-family members when a family member has been designated as the "heir apparent."

PROCEDURE

1. Form groups of four members. After reading the background information about the company and four role players, decide who will play the role of Paula Cale, Robert Fleck, Francesca Sanchez, and Aaron Cale. Review the role description provided by the instructor and prepare to play your role (10 minutes).

Background: Cale Publishing Company was founded by Henry Cale 33 years ago. In recent years, it has been highly successful as a small, independent book publisher, achieving double-digit growth in domestic sales and earnings each year over the last decade. To further its growth, Cale Publishing is considering expansion of its international business by establishing affiliates in other countries, with a first affiliate tentatively to be launched in China. At the same time, questions have been raised about whether the marketing strategy that has fueled the company's domestic successes needs to be adapted to make use of new technologies and be successful in the global market. The CEO has called a meeting to discuss these issues. The following individuals will participate in the meeting:

a. **Paula Cale**, Henry's daughter, has been CEO and Chair of the Board of Directors of Cale Publishing since Henry's death 11 years ago.

b. **Robert Fleck**, a non-family member, is Vice President of Marketing, reports directly to Paula, and has worked at Cale Publishing for 22 years.

c. **Francesca Sanchez**, a non-family member, is Manager of Marketing, reports directly to Robert, and has worked at Cale Publishing for five years.

d. **Aaron Cale**, son of Paula, is the newly appointed Director of Marketing, has a dotted-line reporting relationship to Robert but primarily reports to Paula, has just graduated from the state university with a B.S. in Marketing, and has held summer jobs at Cale Publishing in the past.

2. Hold the meeting. (20–30 minutes)

3. Participate in a discussion based on the following questions: (remaining time)

a. What kinds of underlying problems are present in this situation?

b. How does each person feel in this situation?

c. What should Paula do?

d. Is anyone to blame in this situation?

e. How can this kind of situation be avoided in the future?

REFERENCES   Gersick, K. E., Davis, J. A., Hampton, M. M., & Lansberg, I. (1997). *Generation to generation: Life cycles of the family business.* Boston: Harvard Business School Press.

Habbershon, T. G. (2000). *Improving the long-run survival of family firms: LEADS research project.* Babson Park, MA: Babson College. Retrieved May 3, 2010, from http://www.babson.edu.

Habbershon, T. G., & Pistrui, J. (2002). Enterprising families domain: Family-influenced ownership groups in pursuit of transgenerational wealth. *Family Business Review, 15,* 223–237.

Lansberg, I. (2007). The tests of a prince. *Harvard Business Review, 85*(9), 92–101.

18

Puzzled Perceptions

Purpose:
1. To examine how the Americans with Disabilities Act applies to employment settings.
2. To encourage participants to examine their perceptions of people with disabilities.
3. To examine behavioral dynamics that occur when a disabled employee joins a work team.

Preparation: None

Time: 60 to 75 minutes

BACKGROUND

People with disabilities represent the largest minority group in the United States, and the only one that people can join at any time. Approximately one in six Americans suffers from a disability. Disabilities are generally classified as either visual, auditory, mobility, or cognitive impairments, with the degree of impairment ranging from severely impaired and unable to function without close mainte- nance to able to function successfully in the workplace with modifi- cation of the job, equipment, or work environment. Two-thirds of adults with disabilities are able to and would like to work. However, only about one-third of adults with disabilities are employed.

AUTHOR'S NOTE: This exercise was prepared by Michelle L. Ouimette and Gary N. Powell.

The Americans with Disabilities Act (ADA) addresses the rights of people with disabilities. To be considered a disability under the ADA, a physical or mental impairment must substantially limit one or more major life activities such as seeing, hearing, speaking, walking, breathing, learning, performing manual tasks, or caring for oneself; the individual, however, is otherwise qualified to perform the essential functions of the job. The ADA is intended to protect the rights of people in this category. Employers are required to make a reasonable accommodation when a disabled employee requests one and if it does not constitute an undue hardship to the business. The accommodation should be both necessary for effective job performance by the employee and economically feasible for the employer.

The purpose of this exercise is to help participants understand the impact of the ADA in the employment setting and to examine their own perceptions of disabled people and how to work with them. It is intended to impart knowledge, attitudinal awareness, and skills needed to promote an inclusive work environment for people with disabilities. The exercise simulates an environment in which a new, profoundly disabled employee is introduced to an established team. The team will be successful to the extent that it performs well *and* makes its newest member feel fully included in team processes.

PROCEDURE

1. You are employed by Acme Puzzles, where teams of employees assemble three-dimensional (3D) puzzles. The instructor will divide the class into teams of five to seven members and designate one person from each team to be a newly-hired employee with a disability. The new employees will be asked to gather outside the classroom to await further instruction. (5 minutes)

2. The instructor tells the teams assembled without their new members that a new employee will arrive shortly who has a particular disability. Teams should plan how they will (a) assemble the puzzle as fast as possible and (b) make a reasonable accommodation to the new member that will enable him or her to participate fully in the production process and feel fully included in the team. The instructor will then leave the room to provide instruction to the disabled employees. (10 minutes)

3. The instructor will introduce the new member to each team and give the team an unassembled 3D puzzle along with a picture of the completed puzzle for each member. Tell the instructor when your team has completed the puzzle and provide it for inspection. (maximum of 20 minutes)

4. On a 5-point scale (1 = *strongly disagree*, 5 = *strongly agree*), answer the following questions about how well your team's new member was included in team processes and calculate statistics based on your answers. (10 minutes)

   a. Questions for new team member:

      (1) The team fully included me in its production process.

      (2) People appreciated what I brought to the team.

      (3) I liked being a member of this team.

   Calculate your "inclusion score" as the sum of your answers to these three questions and report it to the instructor.

   b. Questions for other team members:

      (1) We fully included the new team member in our production process.

      (2) I appreciated what the new member brought to the team.

      (3) I liked having the new member on the team.

   Calculate your "inclusion score" as the sum of your answers to these three questions. Then calculate the average of all team members' inclusion scores (other than the new member) and report it to the instructor.

5. Record scores reported by the instructor in the following table:

Team No.	Task Performance		New Member		Other Team Members	
	Assembly Time	Ranking	Inclusion Score	Ranking	Average Inclusion Score	Ranking

6. The instructor will announce the winning team as the one with the lowest (best) sum of the rankings for task performance and new member inclusion score. (5 minutes)

7. Participate in a discussion based on the following questions: (remaining time)

    a. What accommodation did each team make for its disabled member? How well did the accommodation work?

    b. What do the team scores and rankings say about how well members worked as a team?

    c. Were any of the accommodations made by teams unreasonable to expect in the workplace?

    d. What can teams do to make disabled employees feel like full-fledged members?

    e. What do employers need to do to ensure that disabled employees are fully included in the teams to which they are assigned?

REFERENCES

Pati, G. C., & Bailey, E. K. (1995). Empowering people with disabilities: Strategy and human resource issues in implementing the ADA. *Organizational Dynamics, 23*(3), 52–69.

U.S. Department of Labor, Office of Disability Employment Policy. (2003). *Statistics about people with disabilities and employment.* Retrieved December 2, 2003, from http://www.dol.gov.

U.S. Department of Labor, Office of Disability Employment Policy. (2010). *Diversity and disabilities.* Retrieved May 4, 2010, from http://www.dol.gov.

U.S. Equal Employment Opportunity Commission. (2010). *The ADA: Questions and answers.* Retrieved May 4, 2010, from http://www1.eeoc.gov.

19

Sara's Acting Strange Lately

Purpose:
1. To increase awareness of mental illnesses.
2. To examine stereotypes, prejudice, and discrimination involving people with a mental illness.
3. To consider legal and management issues associated with the employment of people with a mental illness.

Preparation: None

Time: 60 to 75 minutes

BACKGROUND

Mental illness describes a broad range of conditions such as schizophrenia, depression, bipolar disorder, obsessive-compulsive disorder, attention deficit/hyperactivity disorder, eating disorders, and anxiety disorders that afflict people of all ages. About one in four adults experiences a mental health disorder, which may be temporary, in a given year, and about one in 17 adults (6%) lives with a serious mental illness. Most mental illnesses are treatable with a combination of medication and psychosocial supports such as counseling and self-help groups. However, because symptoms vary in severity from person to person and do not always follow a regular pattern, it is difficult to predict whether functioning will improve or worsen even if treatment recommendations are followed. While some people require temporary treatment and support, others need

AUTHOR'S NOTE: This exercise was prepared by Susan W. Crisafulli, Michelle J. Morales, Nima A. Patel, Lisa Reigle, and Gary N. Powell.

occasional help when periodic episodes occur, and still others need more substantial and ongoing assistance.

The Americans with Disabilities Act (ADA), which defines a disability as a physical or mental impairment that substantially limits one or more major life activities, bans discrimination against qualified, disabled individuals as long as they can perform the job with a reasonable accommodation that does not impose an undue hardship on the employer. Employers and employees, however, tend to be insensitive to issues raised by mental illness. Although mental illnesses are biologically caused brain disorders, many people associate them with personal weakness. Because the myth prevails that they can just "snap out of it" by choice, people with a mental illness are stigmatized as lacking in will power and character, and they suffer from prejudice and discrimination.

What constitutes a reasonable workplace accommodation for employees with mental illnesses? What can employers do to promote fair and sensitive treatment of such employees? The purpose of this exercise is to examine how employees react to a coworker with a mental illness and to consider management's role in the situation.

PROCEDURE

1. In a prior class, the instructor will select five volunteers to perform a skit.

2. Observe the skit. (20 minutes)

3. Participate in a discussion based on the following questions: (remaining time)

   a. What would constitute a reasonable accommodation to Sara's disability?

   b. How do you believe the manager should have handled the situation?

c. How does the Americans with Disabilities Act apply to this situation?

d. What can employers do to address prejudice toward employees with mental illnesses?

e. What can employees do when prejudice against a coworker with a mental illness is expressed in their presence?

REFERENCES   National Alliance on Mental Illness (NAMI). (2010). *Mental illness: Facts and numbers.* Retrieved May 4, 2010, from http://www.nami.org.
National Alliance on Mental Illness (NAMI). (2010). *What is mental illness: Mental illness facts.* Retrieved May 4, 2010, from http://www.nami.org.

20

The Older Employee

Purpose:
1. To examine attitudes toward older workers.
2. To consider the influence of age-related biases on work relationships among team members.
3. To explore the influence of interoffice communication on preconceived notions of a new employee.

Preparation: None

Time: 60 to 75 minutes

BACKGROUND

The employment rate of older workers (i.e., 50 years old and over) has been rising dramatically in many countries. In the United States, 30% of the labor force consists of older workers, a proportion that has been gradually increasing due to longer life expectancies, financial needs, and the desire to continue working.

In the United States, the Age Discrimination in Employment Act (ADEA) bans discrimination against individuals who are 40 years old and over. In the United Kingdom, the "Age Positive" campaign encourages employers to voluntarily recognize the business benefits of an age-diverse workforce. However, age discrimination is rampant, especially in high-tech industries that value innovation and rapid responsiveness to market demands. Older workers are at a disadvantage in obtaining new jobs or holding onto their present jobs

AUTHOR'S NOTE: This exercise was prepared by Kathleen R. Butterworth, Christopher R. Corcoran, and Gary N. Powell.

during corporate downsizings and restructurings. Managers tend to judge them as weak on flexibility, acceptance of new technology, and ability to learn new skills, all valuable traits in the rapidly changing global economy. Although older workers today are more ready to embrace new technologies than their counterparts in prior generations, the myth persists that "you cannot teach an old dog new tricks."

   If investing in older workers is seen as yielding little in return, corporations will not give older workers the chance to learn the skills they need to stay current in their jobs. The purpose of this exercise is to examine workplace biases faced by older individuals and to consider how organizations can make the work environment both fair and comfortable for workers of all ages.

PROCEDURE

1. Form teams of four to six members. Select one person from each team to play the role of an older employee, Fran Bello, who will be joining the team after it has begun work on a new project. The individuals playing the role of Fran will be asked to gather outside the classroom to await further instruction. The instructor will distribute a background sheet on the team and its new project to all members except Fran; they should review it and then begin work on the project. (10 minutes)

2. As a team, work on the project. (10 minutes)

3. The instructor will distribute an interoffice memo about the new employee. After team members have read it, Fran will join the team. (5 minutes)

4. Continue to work on the project as a team. (20 minutes)

5. Participate in a discussion based on the following questions: (remaining time)

   a. Questions for team members other than Fran Bello:

      (1) What assumptions, if any, did you make upon reading the memo announcing Fran's arrival?

      (2) What was your first impression of Fran?

(3) How did Fran impact your team's effectiveness?

b. Questions for individuals playing the role of Fran Bello:

(1) How did you disclose your skills or lack of skills relevant to the project to the team members?

(2) Did the team respect what you had to offer?

(3) Did you feel fully included as a member of the team?

c. General questions:

(1) How did the team dynamics change after Fran's arrival?

(2) What similar real-life situations have you experienced?

(3) How can employers ensure that older employees are fully included in the teams to which they are assigned?

REFERENCES

Greller, M. M., & Stroh, L. K. (2004). Making the most of "late-career" for employers and workers themselves: Becoming elders not relics. *Organizational Dynamics, 33* (2), 202–214.

Myths about aging: Helping seniors improve with age. (2010). Retrieved May 4, 2010, from http://www.go60.com.

U.K. Department for Work and Pensions. (2009). *Age isn't an issue: An employer's guide to a 21st century workforce.* Retrieved May 4, 2010, from http://www.dwp.gov.uk.

U.S. Department of Labor, Bureau of Labor Statistics. (2010). *Labor force statistics from the Current Population Survey*, table 3. Retrieved May 4, 2010, from http://www.bls.gov/cps.

U.S. Equal Employment Opportunity Commission. (2010). *Age discrimination.* Retrieved May 4, 2010, from http://www1.eeoc.gov.

21 The College Graduate

Purpose:	1. To examine issues that arise when college graduates enter the workplace.
	2. To examine interactions between younger and older employees in work settings.
	3. To examine the influence of physical appearance on workplace interactions.

| *Preparation:* | None |

| *Time:* | 60 to 75 minutes |

BACKGROUND

As stated in the introduction to the previous learning activity, The Older Employee, the Age Discrimination in Employment Act (ADEA) bans discrimination against individuals who are 40 years old and over. However, the ADEA does not protect individuals under the age of 40 who may also be subject to age discrimination.

Several issues may arise when younger workers who are college graduates, especially if they have little work experience, begin their employment. On the one hand, older coworkers as well as coworkers who are less educated may resent their presence and not give them a chance to prove themselves. When a less-experienced recent college graduate is promoted into a management position, more-experienced

AUTHOR'S NOTE: This exercise was prepared by Kevin M. Ladabouche, Daniel R. Mento, Jennifer E. Moter, Stephen C. Potter, Emilia Traina, Casey M. Walsh, and Gary N. Powell.

subordinates who believe that one of their own is more deserving may actively undermine the authority of their new boss. On the other hand, young college graduates may receive inordinate attention from their coworkers, especially if they are regarded as physically attractive. These issues do not always arise, but management needs to be ready to respond when they do.

The purpose of this exercise is to explore such issues, focusing on the effects of age, physical appearance, and education on workplace interactions between college graduates and their older, more experienced, and sometimes less-educated coworkers.

PROCEDURE

1. In a prior class, the instructor will select four or five volunteers to prepare each of three different skits to be performed in front of the class.

2. Observe each skit. (15 minutes for each skit)

3. After each skit, participate in a discussion based on the following questions: (10 minutes for each skit)

    a. What should the college graduate's boss do?

    b. What should the college graduate do?

4. After all skits have been performed and discussed, compare responses to the two discussion questions and identify factors that the college graduate's boss should take into account when responding in such situations. (remaining time)

REFERENCES

Armour, S. (1999, April 20). New kids on the block: Younger bosses raising workplace issues. *USA Today*, A1–A2.

U.S. Equal Employment Opportunity Commission. (2010). *Age discrimination*. Retrieved May 4, 2010, from http://www1.eeoc.gov.

22 Diversity Incidents

Purpose:	1. To examine the managerial implications of having a diverse work force.
	2. To help you deal more effectively with situations in which diversity plays a role.
	3. To distinguish between situations in which discrimination has taken place, situations that have been managed poorly, and situations in which oversensitivity has occurred.
Preparation:	Read and analyze incidents
Time:	60 to 120 minutes

BACKGROUND

Organizations benefit when they **promote nondiscrimination** in treatment of people and decisions about people. This means promoting compliance by all employees with federal, state, and local equal employment opportunity (EEO) laws. Such laws ban discrimination on the basis of sex, race, ethnicity, national origin, age, religion, pregnancy, and other personal characteristics that are not relevant to the job at hand. It also means refraining from discrimination on the basis of job-irrelevant personal characteristics even if it not illegal. For

AUTHOR'S NOTE: This exercise was prepared by John F. Veiga and John N. Yanouzas (#1–8) and Gary N. Powell (#9–16). Incidents #1–8: © John F. Veiga and John N. Yanouzas. Used with permission.

example, there is no U.S. federal law banning discrimination on the basis of sexual orientation, but such discrimination is just as unacceptable as sex or race discrimination. An organization that does a better job of promoting nondiscrimination among employees is less likely to be the target of costly litigation.

Although sometimes it seems that charges of discrimination and lawsuits are rampant, not all claims are warranted. What some see as unfair or illegal discrimination, others see as unwarranted demands for special treatment. In addition, poor management may contribute to perceptions of discrimination that has not actually taken place. The purpose of this exercise is to examine a series of situations, all of which are based on real-life incidents, in which someone feels discriminated against. Considering these situations should give you greater appreciation of the wide range of employee differences that exist and questions of treatment that arise in managing a diverse workforce.

PROCEDURE

1. Prior to class, read the Diversity Incidents and record your preliminary analysis of each on the Analysis page by responding to the following questions:

   a. Has discrimination occurred?

   b. If so, is the discrimination illegal?

   c. Has anyone been the target of prejudice?

   d. Is anyone oversensitive?

   e. Has the situation been managed well or poorly?

2. The instructor will solicit suggestions for incidents to be discussed by the class. (15 minutes per incident)

REFERENCE

Powell, G. N. (2011). Chapter 9, Promoting nondiscrimination, diversity, and inclusion. *Women and men in management*, 4th ed. (pp. 213–240). Thousand Oaks, CA: Sage.

DIVERSITY INCIDENTS

These incidents depict real-life situations. Although they may cause discomfort to some readers, they are not intended to degrade or diminish respect for members of any racial, ethnic, gender, age, religious, or other group.

1. THAT FAT SLOB

Background: The Service Department of Computer Universe maintained the computers of many small and large businesses in the area. The clients who provided the most lucrative contracts were given extra special attention and service. One such client demanded a change in the specialist who serviced its computers.

Computer Service Manager: Fran Stone, the Computer Service Manager, was dumbfounded when a major client demanded that John Zurn be removed from the account. When Fran asked why, the client claimed that John was incompetent. When the client could not elaborate on the incompetence allegation, the true reason emerged. Pushed to the wall, the client said, "That fat slob couldn't service my chair." To avoid the loss of this account, Fran assigned another service specialist to replace John.

Computer Service Specialist: John Zurn took great pride in his work and was pleased with the list of prestigious clients he worked for. He enjoyed his work and got along fine with everyone but was constantly uneasy about his weight. At 5' 8", his weight of 350 pounds was out of control. To help himself bear this cross, John joined the National Association to Advance Fat Acceptance (NAAFA), an association that fights weight-related discrimination and promotes a positive self-image for the targets of such discrimination. He is now convinced more than ever that fat people can be excellent at whatever they do. Fran's decision to remove John from this prestigious account is a serious setback for John's newfound confidence.

2. WHEN IS A "GOOD MORNING" GOOD?

Background: In recent years, university campuses have experienced some of the problems afflicting society in general concerning racial bias and harassment. Students, faculty, administrators, and support staff have been accused of racial discrimination, causing some universities to adopt numerous anti-harassment policies and programs for students as well as faculty aimed at improving racial harmony. But the very effort of trying to define harassment and discrimination in a lively college campus has generated allegations of harassment. A faculty member who was discussing how difficult it is to recognize the subtleties of discrimination and harassment described the following incident that had occurred to a manager:

> "A manager greeted the office staff with a 'Good morning, it is such a nice day.' A Black employee reacted by saying, 'It may be a nice day for you but it isn't for my mother who is freezing in her house in Alabama because she cannot afford to buy heating fuel.'"

The instructor ended the discussion by saying, "Harassment is a subjective matter and we must learn how to define it better." At the end of the instructor's comments, one student left the classroom and returned 15 minutes later. After the session, the student visited the instructor in his office and accused him of engaging in racial discrimination because the incident "made all Blacks look bad."

Instructor: In an effort to make learning more meaningful, the instructor of a management course used experiential methods in the classroom including exercises, role plays, and discussions. Dealing openly with biases and harassment in organizations was clearly integral to the course and discussing it in class was appropriate and legitimate. Ignoring the race of someone in an incident would mask a crucial fact and would not provide relevant information that students needed to confront racial issues and discuss them.

Student: The student came to the university because she hoped to live in an environment free of racial discrimination in contrast to the place she came from. The student felt her request to the instructor to refrain from making Blacks look bad was reasonable. She felt that the instructor was presenting a good course but could do it without demeaning any racial group or offending any student. When the instructor did not yield to her request, she became visibly upset and left the office in disgust.

3. THE CONVICTED FELON

Background: Maxx Candy Company was experiencing a severe shortage of accountants and was urgently trying to fill at least two of its three vacant positions in accounting.

Human Resources Manager: The Human Resources Manager placed ads in all of the appropriate places and received only five applications. The best application was from Betty Whitney, though she had served a short jail sentence for selling narcotics. She had an excellent school record and did a semester's internship in a corporation similar to Maxx. The Human Resources Manager was surprised and perplexed when the Accounting Manager discretely removed Whitney's application.

Accounting Manager: The Accounting Manager realized that the shortage of accountants in the entire region would complicate and lengthen the search, so he pressed the Human Resources Manager hard to get a search mounted. Quarterly reports were due in five weeks and Accounting needed as many hands as possible. The Accounting Manager was impressed with Betty Whitney's credentials until he came to the information on her criminal conviction. Because Maxx is a candy company that sells a product used by children, he could not hire a convicted felon. Besides, he thought, she would never fit in with the rest of the staff.

4. NO HABLA ESPAÑOL, AQUI

Background: Tasty Food Service distributes precooked food to 30 locations in a large city. The workforce and clientele are over 90% Black and Hispanic. Some of the correspondence and advertisements must be done in both English and Spanish. Until recently, the Food Manager hired professional translators to do this work but now is relying on Anna Maria Luz, a bilingual Account Clerk, to translate letters and fliers.

Food Manager: Jane Lessard has been the Food Manager for 20 years and seems to manage effectively though strictly. One of her rules is "English only in the office." Troubled by Anna Maria, who frequently converses in Spanish with other employees, the Food Manager told her to stop violating the English-only rule. Jane believes that Hispanics should be forced to learn the language of their adopted land. After all, she thinks, this is a one-language country. Anna Maria's reaction was to go into a slowdown with Jane's requests for translation work.

Account Clerk: Even though it was not in her job description, doing the translation work did not bother Anna Maria until Jane clamped down on the English-only rule. Because Jane expected Anna Maria to engage in Spanish translations, she felt that Jane should not require her to abide by this rule. Furthermore, Anna Maria felt that some of the Hispanics could do better work if instructions were in Spanish.

5. WHY ME?

Background: Chase Memorial Hospital, a progressive 1,000-bed teaching facility, has introduced a "clinical ladder and merit system" to provide an orderly way for nurses to be promoted based on merit. For instance, to be promoted to Clinical II Registered Nurse (RN), one must do a self-evaluation and complete a research project or implement a program appropriate to the needs of patients. To help newly hired nurses prepare themselves for promotion, each one is assigned to a mentor, frequently a nurse with more than two years' experience. The clinical ladder and merit system makes it easier to recruit new nurses and retain existing personnel. The head nurse of a unit assigns mentors to new nurses.

Head Nurse: Anne Capp, RN, head nurse of a 27-bed oncology unit, is a graduate from the outdated Chase School of Nursing diploma program but is currently working part time on a bachelor's degree. Although she's a traditionalist, Anne's technical skills and bedside manner are up-to-date. Since the oncology unit is staffed by young, well-trained, and ambitious people, the head nurse maintains a proper distance from the staff but believes she is fair and accessible. Understanding young people, however, is the most difficult part of her job. For instance, she cannot understand why a Black nurse, Esther Wilson, balked at becoming the mentor for a newly hired Black nurse.

Nurse: Esther Wilson has made good progress in her two years at Chase, but she has fallen behind in preparing her proposal for a special interest program—developing a network of providers for family-centered home care of cancer patients. For two years, Anne treated her like a competent nurse, but now Esther feels she is being singled out as a Black nurse. Assigning her to be mentor to a newly hired Black nurse was done without even consulting her. Esther was reluctant to decline the assignment, but it has slowed her progress. This will delay her eligibility to become Clinical II RN.

6. ALL WORK AND NO PLAY

Background: A group of newly hired accountants has just completed the introductory training program in the Audit Department of Peat, Ernst, and Deloitte in New York City. Audit managers assign new auditors to specific clients. Matching up auditors to managers and clients is never done to the satisfaction of all parties. Darren Young, one of the newly trained auditors, has complained that he was not assigned any of the clients he had hoped to get and suspects that one of the audit managers, Hank Roberts, is biased in selecting a single female to work for him and many of the clients Darren wanted.

Audit Manager: Hank Roberts had an opportunity to survey the new auditors when he was the instructor for three days during their training session. He really hit it off well with Cathy Terio because she was a good auditor and also liked to party after class. Hank believes that with so many young, single people in the profession, one of the perks for working in New York City is the opportunity to combine work with fun. Otherwise why put up with all of the stresses of working in New York City?

Auditor: Darren is a bright, pleasant, reserved, and ambitious young accountant who deliberately elected to work in New York after he graduated from a Mormon university in Utah. He wanted to work with the best and brightest colleagues and for a wide array of impressive clients. When he learned that Cathy Terio got the assignments he wanted, Darren reasoned that nonwork criteria, such as partying, having fun, and drinking after work, were more important than his sound qualifications and work ethic. Why should lifestyle enter into assignment decisions?

7. THE TOP FIVE CLUB

Background: Kidwell Investments, a large brokerage house, recently moved into the most prestigious office building in Hartford, Connecticut. To take advantage of the publicity associated with the building, Kidwell ran a full-page promotional advertisement in the *Hartford Daily Times*. It showed the five top brokers in the office in terms of sales production sitting around a U-shaped table, with related copy emphasizing stability, reliability, and dedication. All of these brokers were White males. The ad had an immediate impact in terms of increased sales for the brokers pictured. However, it also caused some grumbling, particularly from brokers who did not benefit directly. Rebecca Moore, a high-producing broker, was especially upset.

Vice President: Frank Casey, resident vice president, personally handled the promotional ad and selected the top five brokers because he felt that they presented an image of dependable, high-quality financial service. Frank thought that no matter how many people were selected to be in the ad, others who were not pictured would complain.

Broker: Rebecca Moore made rapid progress in Kidwell and had the sixth best sales record in the office. Her clients include both male and female investors. In her eyes, the old myth about women not being good money handlers was dying fast. To her, the ad looked as if it was a picture taken in a men's-only club. She feels that Frank deliberately selected the top five to keep a female face out of the ad.

8. SIESTA TIME

Background: An American firm operating a bakery on the U.S. side of the border with Mexico is experiencing difficulties applying U.S. work standards and management practices to Mexicans who come across the border daily to work. Edward Tippett, an American foreman in the truck maintenance and repair shop, is regularly bothered by incidents that he feels would never happen with American workers. All of the employees except Tippett are Mexican. The most troublesome mechanic is Ramon Ramos.

Foreman: Edward Tippett supervises eight mechanics, most of whom are good workers, but Ramon Ramos makes up for the others. He is good but careless, ignores basic safety rules, and insists on making up his own schedule. Often, Ramon eats his lunch during work hours and then takes a siesta during the 20-minute lunch break, except the siesta sometimes lasts for 30 or 40 minutes. This disrupts teamwork and is a violation of the work rules. Ed sees this as part of a casual work attitude that Mexicans bring with them when they cross the border. He believes that Americans did not get ahead by sleeping away the afternoons.

Mechanic: Ramon Ramos is a good mechanic who drives across the border daily to earn twice as much as he would in Mexico. He likes his work, even though at times some of the American expectations on work habits go against all that is Mexican. For instance, the siesta is something that all Mexicans observe. However, when they cross the border, the Americans demand that these cultural mores be left behind. The Americans like to hire Mexicans, pay them far less than they would pay locals, and then expect the Mexicans to behave like Americans. Anyway, Ramos feels he works extra hard and makes up during work time the extra 10 minutes that he spends on his siesta.

9. LYING DOWN ON THE JOB

Background: An assistant professor of management in her third year of an initial three-year appointment was reappointed for another three years. However, the university's personnel committee, consisting of elected faculty members from different disciplines, wrote in her letter of reappointment that she needed to work on improving her teaching performance. The same committee will decide whether or not to grant her tenure during the last year of her second three-year appointment.

Assistant Professor: Jane Mangalo was extremely angered by the negative reference to her teaching performance in the letter of reappointment. She had received excellent ratings from students in all but one semester. During that semester, she was pregnant and suffered back pain that made it impossible for her to stand or sit for extended periods of time. The pregnancy prevented her from taking pain-relieving medication. In addition, she was forced to teach while lying on her side on a bench in front of the classroom. This prevented her from writing on the blackboard, her usual practice, as she led case discussions. The back problem went away after she had the baby. However, some students complained about how she taught the class that semester. Jane believed that she did the university a favor by teaching rather than going on disability leave and that the negative reference to her teaching performance in the letter of reappointment constituted discrimination against the disabled.

Personnel Committee: When the personnel committee found evidence of weak teaching performance by Jane in some of her courses, it decided to include in the letter of reappointment the standard language used in such cases, encouraging her to work on improving her teaching performance, while still reappointing her for another three years. When it wrote the letter, the committee was aware of Jane's condition during the sole semester in which the evidence of weak teaching performance appeared. However, it decided not to take into account or make reference to her condition in its letter in the interest of treating all faculty members with similar variation in teaching performance alike.

10. CHANGE AT THE DAILY PLANET

Background: Copy editors for a large metropolitan newspaper work at computer terminals that are located in an open newsroom. Currently, terminals are assigned only to supervisors—copy editors are free to use any open terminal. Almost all of the Black copy editors regularly use terminals in a corner of the newsroom that is distant from supervisors. Tim Olsen, the managing editor, recently announced that copy editors will soon be assigned to terminals near their supervisors. The announced reason for the change is to "improve communications" in the newsroom, but the real reason is to cut down on phone abuse. Tim believes that most of the copy editors who occupy the corner are making personal phone calls on company time. Because it is difficult to document an individual's phone usage when employees can sit anywhere and use any phone, assigning terminals will allow copy editors to be managed more closely and cut down on this kind of abuse.

    White Copy Editor: Doris Lane is strongly opposed to assigned seating. She has always been an outstanding performer. In fact, she recently received an "employee of the year" award from top management. Right now, she regularly sits beside Kerri White, who has become a close friend. Under the proposed change, she may end up sitting beside someone she likes less (such as Mark Kent) and enjoy her job less as a result. Besides, copy editors don't need to sit beside each other to communicate; everyone uses e-mail freely throughout the newsroom.

    Black Copy Editor: Mark Kent is angry about the upcoming change to assigned seating. He likes to sit with his friends, people who see things the way he does. Why should he be forced to sit beside someone like Doris Lane, whom he respects as a copy editor but with whom he personally feels uncomfortable? The real reason for the change is not to "improve communications"; it's because White supervisors feel threatened any time Black employees choose to congregate by themselves. As far as Mark is concerned, this change amounts to racial discrimination.

11. THE GAY BAR

Background: Dale, the owner of an upscale gay bar, was hiring a new bartender. The two best candidates were Rusty (male) and Phyllis (female). Rusty had excellent bartending references from former employers and had a very masculine appearance, but Dale sensed some homophobia on Rusty's part in the interview. Phyllis, who had a nice appearance and was very open about being a lesbian, had previous experience as a waitress but little as a bartender. Dale felt that even though Rusty had outstanding bartender credentials, his attitude toward homosexuality was an obstacle. Dale hired Phyllis.

    Male Applicant: Rusty had been a bartender for 10 years, working his way up to head bartender at a fancy sports bar. He was proud of his ability to mix any drink, including the kind that could "knock the ears of a tough hombre," without referring to the manual. Customers always seemed to be amused by his vast knowledge and anecdotes. Now he found himself living in another city and in need of a job. Working at a gay bar was not his top choice, but it was the best of all of his alternatives. He applied for the position at Dale's bar but was rejected in favor of a woman. Rusty visited Dale's bar and saw for himself that the woman who got the job didn't know much about mixed drinks. Based on what he observed, Rusty decided to lodge a sex discrimination complaint against Dale.

Owner: Rusty's bartending credentials were impressive. However, Dale sensed some uneasiness when he talked with Rusty about the bar's clientele. While Rusty did not admit to being homophobic, he did make it clear that he was straight. Although Dale believes that sexual orientation is a personal matter, he concluded that Rusty would have difficulty dealing with an all-gay clientele because of his underlying attitude toward homosexuality.

12. A TOUCH OF CLASS

Background: The superintendent of schools in a small New England town received an anonymous e-mail message stating that the middle school principal is a co-owner of an adult "swingers" club that meets in a neighboring town. Several media outlets also received the anonymous e-mail. Circulation of this news caused a considerable public outcry. The superintendent asked the principal to resign after the principal confirmed that she was a co-owner of the club. When the principal refused, the superintendent fired her.

Superintendent: Charles Berry, superintendent of schools in Pleasantville, felt caught in the middle. Janice Wakefield was an excellent principal who was dedicated to the students. The sensationalized media reports, however, had townspeople demanding that action be taken. One angry citizen wrote, "The principal's part-ownership of a sex club is morally wrong, and it's a poor example for the children. The high school students are reading about it in the newspaper, and the younger students are seeing it on TV. The purpose of the schools is to educate our children, and this is both distracting and offensive." Another parent called him to state, "Whether you are a school board member, principal, teacher, or in any other role in the public schools, when you are put in the public eye, you have to be clean." A group of parents with children in the school system even threatened to petition for the superintendent's ouster if he did not remove Janice. He felt he had no choice but to do what he did.

Principal: Janice Wakefield, principal of the Pleasantville Middle School, was outraged that media broadcasts of her private life were costing her a job she loved and possibly her career. She and her husband have two children and are co-owners of A Touch of Class, an upscale, members-only, adult lifestyles club for couples with a sense of adventure. The club, which is perfectly legal and does not violate any town or state regulations, meets in an 11-room, Queen Anne–style Victorian house with dual fireplaces every Friday and Saturday night. Club members are discreet and do not disturb the neighbors. As far as Janice is concerned, it's just like a bunch of people who get together and play pool except for the activity they are conducting. So why should it be anybody else's business? Janice's excellent evaluations for her work first as a teacher and then as a principal in the Pleasantville school system didn't count in her favor once an old-fashioned witch-hunt got started.

13. THIS JOB STINKS

Background: Mandy, a paralegal at a law firm, complains that various smells in the office aggravate her migraine headaches. Threatening to file a complaint, Mandy leaves the office early several days a week. Her latest protest is that Jane, an administrative assistant who is seated three cubicles away, cleaned her desk with a chemical that intensified the migraine. The day before, Mandy claimed that Jane was wearing too much perfume. On both days, Mandy left early, saying that the smells made it impossible for her to work. Pete, the head attorney, has noticed that people are constantly cleaning their desks and wearing a lot of perfume lately.

   Administrative Assistant: Jane's desk was getting dusty, so she used a company-supplied cleaning solution to clean it. She didn't see how Mandy, who works three cubicles away, could have been adversely affected. Based on Mandy's prior complaints, Jane stopped wearing perfume to the office; however, Mandy still accused her of wearing too much perfume. Jane was appalled by Mandy's behavior. It seemed clear that Mandy was fabricating excuses to leave the office early. Jane didn't understand why the head attorney wasn't addressing this issue.

   Paralegal: Mandy gets migraine headaches frequently. Her doctor told her that strong smells could intensify the pain. Mandy believes that people should limit the amount of perfume they wear or avoid cleaning their desks until after she has left. She doesn't want to file a complaint, but she can no longer work under these conditions. The other workers are starting to resent her, and she thinks that they are cleaning their desks more frequently and wearing an inordinate amount of perfume on purpose.

14. A PIERCING ISSUE

Background: Jessica Lobo, 22 years old, was an employee of Edges, a popular bookstore and cafe located near the campus of a major university. After she had worked at the bookstore for almost a year, the owner, Charles Belaga, implemented a new dress code on facial jewelry that allowed only one facial piercing in addition to ear piercing. Jessica had worn multiple items of facial jewelry ever since she began working at Edges. She refused to comply with the new dress code and was fired.

   Employee: Jessica did not see why she should remove almost all of her facial jewelry (a nose ring, three lip and three tongue studs, two eyebrow rings). Before the owner told her about the new policy, Jessica had earned praise and promotions during her year at the store. She does not understand what this has to do with her job performance. Her body piercing is not just part of her wardrobe, it also represents her spiritual beliefs. Each piercing marks a period of history in her life. She feels that the new dress code on facial jewelry curtails her freedom to express herself and is discriminatory.

   Owner: Charles knew that he was within his rights to implement a dress code and felt that it was perfectly reasonable. He believes that the appearance of Edges employees reflects the image of the bookstore and customers' perceptions of it. If Jessica does not want to adhere to the dress code, that's her choice, but she should not expect to remain a bookstore employee. After all, Edges has an image to uphold.

15. QUIT DRIVING UP MY HEALTH CARE COSTS

Background: Blake Products, a manufacturer of metal tools, recently increased employee contributions to health care premiums, citing rising costs. Noting that a few serious illnesses can increase the cost of coverage for everyone, the company urged employees to monitor their health and it implemented several health-related initiatives. For example, a diet expert taught classes about the benefits of avoiding fatty foods, and supervisors were encouraged to discuss with workers how the bad habits of some lead to higher costs for all. Since Blake Products took these actions, some workers have been taunting others about health-related issues.

Machine Operator: Since he was diagnosed with heart disease, David Johnson, age 58, has become a devout vegetarian and has gone from size-40 to size-32 pants. He sees nothing wrong with criticizing coworkers like Eugene White when he sees them carrying bags of junk food. He tells them to read the ingredients and think about the poisons they are chomping down. After all, why should he have to pay for others who are not taking care of themselves?

Fork Lift Driver: Eugene White, age 58, 6 feet tall, and 340 pounds, knows that he is obese but is sick and tired of coworkers' taunts about his weight. Just last week, he heard David Johnson, also 58, say loudly as he was driving by, "Just look at that guy, his belly's almost touching the steering wheel. It's gross." Eugene feels that he should not have to put up with this harassment and has complained to his boss about it. So far, management appears unsympathetic. They are too busy coming up with new ways to harangue workers about their weight to care.

16. YOU'RE FIRED

Background: Jane McMahon was a single pre-kindergarten teacher at East-West Catholic School. After Jane informed Terry Jennings, the school's principal, that she was pregnant and planned to have the child, she was fired for violating Catholic morality. Jane's pregnancy was evidence that she engaged in premarital sex, which is forbidden under the teachings of Roman Catholicism.

Teacher: Jane and her boyfriend Tom did not intend to have children until after they were married. When Jane found out that she was pregnant, abortion was not an option because both she and Tom are Catholic. She feels betrayed by the principal's decision, which directly followed a very positive performance review. In fact, the principal wrote in her termination letter, "Your teaching ability and love of your children was of a high degree of professionalism." If she was fired for having premarital sex, why doesn't the school or diocese enforce this policy against men? She regards her firing as blatant sex discrimination, and hypocritical to boot.

Principal: Parents send their children to East-West Catholic School for both educational and moral development. When Terry was told that Jane was pregnant, her heart sank. As principal of East-West, she was torn in two directions. Jane was an exceptional young teacher who has a great deal of potential. She had done a great job of establishing rapport with the pre-kindergartners. Ironically, that's what made it impossible to avoid firing her. The school's personnel handbook states that "a teacher is required to convey the teachings of the Catholic faith by his or her words and actions, demonstrating an acceptance of Gospel values and the Christian tradition." As the world becomes more secular, it is hard to ensure that students uphold traditional Catholic values, particularly abstinence. Having her most popular teacher walking around the school pregnant and unwed would make Terry's job even more difficult.

DIVERSITY INCIDENTS

ANALYSIS

Instructions: Respond "yes" or "no" to each question for each incident.

Diversity Incident	*Discrimination?*	*If discrimination, is it illegal?*	*Prejudice?*	*Oversensitivity?*	*Managed well or poorly?*
1. That Fat Slob					
2. When Is a "Good Morning" Good?					
3. The Convicted Felon					
4. No Habla Español, Aqui					
5. Why Me?					
6. All Work and No Play					
7. The Top Five Club					
8. Siesta Time					
9. Lying Down on the Job					
10. Change at the Daily Planet					
11. The Gay Bar					
12. A Touch of Class					
13. This Job Stinks					
14. A Piercing Issue					
15. Quit Driving Up My Health Care Costs					
16. You're Fired					

23 Affirmative Action at Ole State

Purpose:	1. To examine the legal mandate for affirmative action.
	2. To evaluate how affirmative action programs promote diversity in educational settings.
	3. To consider the implications of preferential treatment for members of different groups in college admission decisions.
Preparation:	Complete questionnaire
Time:	60 to 75 minutes

BACKGROUND

Organizations benefit when they **promote diversity** among employees in all jobs and at all levels. The focus of promoting diversity is on the number or *quantity* of employees from various groups in different jobs and at different organizational levels. Affirmative action programs, which are legally mandated for most employers, represent attempts to ensure that organizational practices enhance the employment, development, and retention of members of protected groups such as women and people of color. Organizations also may attempt to increase the diversity of their labor force for business reasons.

Several economic trends suggest that it is advantageous for organizations to promote diversity. First, the labor force has become more diverse in recent years. In most countries, it has become more heterogeneous on the basis of sex, race, ethnicity, national origin, religion, and many other dimensions of diversity. Organizations with

AUTHOR'S NOTE: This exercise was prepared by Gary N. Powell.

management practices appropriate for a homogeneous group of employees need to rethink their human resource management strategies.

Second, the relative skills that members of different groups bring to the workplace have changed. In particular, the educational attainment of female entrants relative to that of male entrants has risen dramatically. Within all racial/ethnic groups in the United States, women now constitute the majority of individuals who earn bachelor's and master's degrees across all disciplines; the proportion of women earning these degrees has increased in many other countries as well. As a result, more women worldwide are prepared to enter the high-paying occupations that require advanced degrees. Organizations that promote diversity by attracting highly educated women to historically male-intensive jobs and occupations are at an advantage in competing with organizations that do not.

Third, there has been a worldwide shift from a primarily manufacturing-based economy to an economy based more on the delivery of services. Service industries place greater importance on educational attainment and less on physical strength than do manufacturing industries. Service firms that aggressively promote diversity may be especially effective in the marketplace. Because services are both produced and consumed on the spot, employees have heightened contact with customers. As the pool of potential customers becomes more diverse, the pool of employees with customer contact also needs to become more diverse for the organization to be successful.

Fourth, the increasing globalization of business, including multinational business operations and worldwide marketing of products and services, calls for organizations to be responsive to customers who are increasingly diverse in national origin.

In the same vein, many colleges and universities assert that educational benefits are derived from a diverse student body. Major businesses have made it clear that the skills needed in the global marketplace can only be developed by exposing students to widely diverse people, cultures, ideas, and viewpoints. The procedures used to promote student diversity have received close legal scrutiny. For example, the U.S. Supreme Court struck down the University of Michigan's undergraduate admission policy, which awarded a specific number of points to all applicants from an underrepresented racial/ethnic group. The Court, however, upheld the university's law school admission policy of assessing all applicants' credentials and abilities on a flexible scale while seeking to enroll a critical mass of underrepresented minority students, arguing that its narrowly tailored use of race in admission decisions served a compelling interest in obtaining the educational benefits that flow from a diverse student body.

The whole notion of affirmative action, whether in business, government, or academe, arouses strong emotions. Increasing the chances that members of one group will experience more favorable outcomes than members of another group is often objected to as "reverse discrimination." Colleges and universities, however, grant preferential treatment in admission decisions to members of some groups (e.g., children of alumni, prior donors, or potential donors) even though there is no legal mandate and it does not address past discrimination. The purpose of this exercise is to examine affirmative action in an educational context by exploring the role of various factors in college admission decisions.

PROCEDURE

1. Prior to class, complete the questionnaire that follows.

2. Form teams of five to seven people. (5 minutes)

3. As a team, complete the questionnaire. (30 minutes)

4. Participate in a discussion of the following questions: (remaining time)

   a. What is your committee's admission policy and the rationale for it?

   b. What types of special treatment were implemented?

   c. What types of special treatment would be illegal?

   d. Do affirmative action programs necessarily lead to reverse discrimination?

   e. Is a diverse student body an appropriate goal for colleges and universities? If so, how can this goal be best achieved?

REFERENCE

Powell, G. N. (2011). Chapter 9, Promoting nondiscrimination, diversity, and inclusion. *Women and men in management*, 4th ed. (pp. 213–240). Thousand Oaks, CA: Sage.

AFFIRMATIVE ACTION AT OLE STATE

QUESTIONNAIRE

You are a member of the undergraduate admission committee for Ole State University, the top public university in your state. Ole State admits about 5,000 undergraduate students each year. It fields teams in over 20 Division I intercollegiate sports, including Division I-A football. Your committee may give special treatment in admission decisions to applicants from many different groups. In establishing your admission policy, answer the following questions.

1. Which of the following groups, if any, should receive special treatment in admission decisions?

    a. Applicants from particular racial/ethnic groups that are underrepresented at the university compared with the population of the state:

        (1) Blacks?

        (2) Hispanics?

        (3) Asians?

        (4) Native Americans?

        (5) Non-Hispanic Whites?

    b. Applicants with a disability covered by the Americans with Disabilities Act?

    c. Applicants from particular geographical locations:

        (1) State residents?

        (2) Residents of other states?

        (3) Residents of other countries?

    d. Military veterans?

    e. Ole State employees?

    f. Children of:

        (1) Alumni?

        (2) Past donors? (If yes, at what level of contribution?)

        (3) Legislators and other key state officials?

        (4) Poor parents who are economically disadvantaged?

        (5) Wealthy parents who are considered potential major donors?

        (6) Ole State employees?

    g. Athletes:

        (1) In high-profile intercollegiate sports that generate net revenues for Ole State?

        (2) In other intercollegiate sports?

    h. Applicants with particular academic qualifications:

        (1) Valedictorian of their graduating class?

      (2) In the top 5% of their graduating class?

      (3) Perfect grade point average (GPA)?

      (4) Perfect SAT score?

      (5) Special creative talents (e.g., won piano competition, received prize for science fair project)?

      (6) Participation in extracurricular activities?

      (7) Leadership role in school or community?

    i. Applicants from any other group? (specify)

2. What type of treatment would you give to members of each group you identified as deserving of special treatment from the above list?

    a. Guaranteed admission.

    b. Guaranteed admission if minimum academic requirements met (e.g., minimum GPA, SAT score, or rank in graduating class).

    c. Specified number of spaces in entering class if minimum academic requirements met (e.g., as typically done for athletes on scholarships).

    d. Specified proportion of spaces in entering class if minimum academic requirements met.

    e. Specified number of points added to application evaluation score.

    f. Other (specify):

24

The Inclusive Workplace

Purpose:	1. To consider the merits of an inclusive workplace culture.
	2. To explore how individuals and groups experience an inclusive culture.
	3. To identify factors—individual, interpersonal, group, intergroup, organizational, and societal—that create and foster an inclusive culture.
Preparation:	None
Time:	60 to 75 minutes

BACKGROUND

Finally, organizations benefit when they **promote inclusion** of employees from all groups in the organizational culture. The focus of promoting inclusion is on the nature or *quality* of work relationships between employees who belong to different groups. There are no laws that say that organizations ought to provide a work environment in which members of all groups feel comfortable and accepted. Organizations may engage in this kind of action if they see some advantage to doing so.

AUTHOR'S NOTE: This exercise was prepared by Bernardo M. Ferdman. © Bernardo M. Ferdman. Used with permission.

Taking steps to promote diversity, but ignoring the need for inclusion, may limit an organization's ability to reap the full benefits of a diverse workforce. Although increased employee diversity may enhance organizational performance, it also poses potential problems. It is easier to maintain a sense of cohesiveness in homogeneous organizations than in diverse organizations. People tend to be more attracted to and feel more comfortable in social settings in which they interact primarily with people like themselves. Thus, diversity may be a double-edged sword, increasing decision-making creativity and the congruence of the organization with the marketplace but decreasing employees' satisfaction with being a member of the organization. Unless the potential problems associated with diversity are addressed, its potential benefits may not be fully realized. The organization's diversity culture, as demonstrated by how it deals with group differences, influences the extent to which these problems appear.

Three types of diversity cultures have been identified. **Monolithic organizations** are characterized by a large majority of employees from one group (e.g., White men), especially in the managerial ranks. Differences between majority and minority group members are resolved by the process of assimilation, whereby minority group employees are expected to adopt the norms and values of the majority group to survive in the organization. Such organizations are characterized by low levels of intergroup conflict because there are few members of minority groups and these members have outwardly adopted, if not inwardly embraced, the majority's norms and values. Changes in workforce demographics have led to a reduction in the number of monolithic organizations with White male majorities. The diversity culture of monolithic organizations conveys a straightforward message to employees and potential job applicants: We do not particularly welcome diversity.

Plural organizations have a more heterogeneous workforce than do monolithic organizations, primarily because they have taken steps to promote diversity. These steps may include hiring and promotion policies that stress recruitment and advancement of members of minority groups and managerial training on equal opportunity issues. Plural organizations focus on the numbers of majority versus minority group members in different jobs and levels, not on the quality of work relationships between members of different groups. The primary approach to resolving cultural differences in plural organizations is assimilation, just as for monolithic organizations. Intergroup conflict is high in plural organizations if members of the majority group resent practices used to boost minority group membership. Even though overt discrimination may have been banished, prejudice is still likely in plural organizations. The diversity culture of plural organizations conveys a mixed message: We promote diversity, but we expect employees from minority groups to fit in with the majority group.

Multicultural organizations do more than promote diversity; they also promote a culture of inclusion. They respond to cultural differences by encouraging members of different groups to respect the norms and values of other groups, in contrast to the assimilation required by monolithic and plural organizations. Multicultural organizations attempt to bring about qualitative changes in their work environments through increased appreciation of the range of skills and values that dissimilar employees offer and increased use of teams that include members culturally distinct from the dominant group. The goal is to create a culture in which employees from all groups feel comfortable and appreciated and are given a chance to make meaningful contributions. In an inclusive culture, the knowledge, skills, insights, and experiences of employees from different groups are regarded as valuable resources that the organization may use to advance its mission. Intergroup conflict in multicultural organizations is low due to the absence of prejudice and discrimination accompanied by the appreciation of individuals from different groups. The diversity culture of multicultural organizations conveys a consistent message: We welcome members of all groups as full participants in our organizational culture, and we strive to take full advantage of what they have to offer.

The purpose of this exercise is to draw upon participants' personal experiences to consider what it takes to create a diversity culture that is truly inclusive. Ideally, it will provide a powerful learning experience that leaves participants energized and eager to implement its lessons long after the course is over.

PROCEDURE   1. Find a partner who is different from you on at least two dimensions of diversity. (5 minutes)

2. Interview each other, addressing the following questions: (20 minutes)

    a. Think of a time at work or school when you felt highly valued, included, and productive; when you drew upon most if not all of yourself as a resource; and when you felt fully energized and alive. What were some highlights of the experience? What made it possible? What did you feel? What did others do and how did their behavior foster these feelings?

    b. Describe one or two key factors in organizations that would make such experiences more likely for you and others.

    c. Make three wishes for how organizations should function in the future.

3. Form eight-member groups by combining four pairs of interview partners. In your group, discuss interview data and extract key themes. (20 minutes)

4. As a class, answer the following questions as many times as possible. (remaining time)

   a. What can organizations do to promote an inclusive workplace?

   b. What can I do to promote an inclusive workplace?

REFERENCES   Cox, T., Jr. (1991). The multicultural organization. *Academy of Management Executive, 5*(2), 34–47.

Holvino, E., Ferdman, B. F., & Merrill-Sands, D. (2004). Creating and sustaining diversity and inclusion in organizations: Strategies and approaches. In M. S. Stockdale & F. J. Crosby (Eds.), *The psychology and management of workplace diversity* (pp. 245–276). Oxford, UK: Blackwell.

Powell, G. N. (2011). Chapter 9, Promoting nondiscrimination, diversity, and inclusion. *Women and men in management,* 4th ed. (pp. 213–240). Thousand Oaks, CA: Sage.

About the Author

Gary N. Powell, Ph.D., is Professor of Management and Director of the Ph.D. Program in the School of Business at the University of Connecticut. He is author of *Women and Men in Management* (4th ed.) and editor of *Handbook of Gender and Work*. He is an internationally recognized scholar and educator on gender and diversity issues in the workplace. His graduate course on women and men in management won an award on innovation in education from the Committee on Equal Opportunity for Women of the American Assembly of Collegiate Schools of Business (AACSB). A subsequent version of the course on managing a diverse workforce, taught at both the graduate and undergraduate level, inspired the preparation of this book. He has won the University of Connecticut School of Business Outstanding Graduate Teaching Award (three times) and Outstanding Undergraduate Teaching Award. He also has received the University of Connecticut President's Award for Promoting Multiculturalism.

He has served as Chair, Program Chair, and Executive Committee member of the Women in Management (now Gender and Diversity in Organizations) Division of the Academy of Management, and received both the Janet Chusmir Service Award for his contributions to the division and the Sage Scholarship Award for his contributions to research on gender in organizations. He has published over 100 articles in journals such as *Academy of Management Journal, Academy of Management Review, Journal of Applied Psychology, Organizational Behavior and Human Decision Processes, Journal of Management, Personnel Psychology, Human Relations, Journal of Organizational Behavior, Organizational Dynamics,* and *Academy of Management Executive;* contributed over 20 chapters to edited volumes; and presented 130 papers at professional conferences. He is a Fellow of the British Academy of Management and Eastern Academy of Management. He has served on the Board of Governors of the Academy of Management and as President and Program Chair of the Eastern Academy of Management. He also served as Co-Chair of the Status of Minorities Task Force of the Academy of Management and has served on the Editorial Board of *Academy of Management Review, Academy of Management Executive, Journal of Management, Human Relations,* and *Journal of Management Studies.*

Prior to joining the faculty at the University of Connecticut, he worked at General Electric, graduating from its Manufacturing Management Program. At GE, he designed and implemented automated project scheduling systems as well as systems for inventory control, materials procurement, and so on. He has provided management training and development for many companies, including Webster Financial Corp., The Hartford Financial Services Group, The Implementation Partners (TIP), GE-Capital, General Signal, Apple Computer, Monroe Auto Equipment, AllState, and CIGNA, and has conducted numerous other workshops.

He holds a doctorate in organizational behavior and a master's degree in management science from the University of Massachusetts, and a bachelor's degree in management from MIT.

SAGE Research Methods Online
The essential tool for researchers

An expert research tool

- An **expertly designed taxonomy** with more than 1,400 unique terms for social and behavioral science research methods

- **Visual and hierarchical search tools** to help you discover material and link to related methods

- Easy-to-use navigation tools
- Content organized by complexity
- Tools for citing, printing, and downloading content with ease
- Regularly updated content and features

A wealth of essential content

- The most comprehensive picture of quantitative, qualitative, and mixed methods available today

- More than **100,000 pages of SAGE book and reference material** on research methods as well as editorially selected material from SAGE journals

- More than **600 books** available in their entirety online

Launching 2011!

$SAGE research methods online